CURRENT AFRICAN ISSUES 37

Migration in sub-Saharan Africa

Aderanti Adepoju

NORDISKA AFRIKAINSTITUTET, UPPSALA 2008

A background paper commissioned by the Nordic Africa Institute
for the Swedish Government White Paper on Africa

INDEXING TERMS:
International migration
Emigration
Economic aspects
Migration policy
Development research
International cooperation
Brain drain
Diaspora
Human trafficking
Africa south of Sahara

The opinions expressed in this volume are those of the author
and do not necessarily reflect the views of the Nordic Africa Institute.

Language checking: Peter Colenbrander
ISSN 0280-2171
ISBN 978-91-7106-620-6
© The author and Nordiska Afrikainstitutet 2008
Printed in Sweden by Elanders Sverige AB, Mölnlycke 2008.

CONTENTS

Abbreviations and acronyms 6

1. Why focus on migration? 7
Introduction 7
Migration – an international agenda 7
Report of the Global Commission on International Migration 7
The African Union's strategic framework for a policy on migration 8
The African Union's common position on migration and development 9
The 2006 Euro-African conference on migration and development 9
The Joint Africa-EU Declaration on Migration and Development 10
The follow-up meeting to the Rabat Process 10
The EU-Africa strategic partnership – The Lisbon Summit 11
The UN High-level Dialogue on Migration and Development 11
The Global Forum on Migration and Development 12

2. The sub-Saharan African migration scene 13
Emigration dynamics: some root causes 13
Migration or circulation? 14
Internal migration 15
Internal migration blends into international migration 17
Migration patterns in sub-Saharan Africa: some historical trends 17
Trends in the stock of international migration in sub-Saharan Africa 19
Recent trends in patterns of migration in and from SSA 21
Diversification of destinations 21
Commercial migration 21
The lure of South Africa and problems of irregular migration 22
The Maghreb – a region of origin, transit and destination 22
Increase in independent female migration 24
A new developmental approach to migration 27
Migration to rich countries 28

3. Emigration of professionals: causes and consequences 29
Brain drain: its determinants and magnitude 29
Impact of the brain drain 31
Measures by donor communities to counter negative effects 33
Brain circulation and skills circulation 34

4. The characteristics and roles of remittances in sub-Saharan Africa 36
Use of remittances 36

  Remittances: micro-meso-macro levels 36
  Remittance policy measures 37
  Transaction costs and incentives 37
  Remittances and development 38

5. The role of the diaspora in country-of-origin development 40
  Diaspora's economic and technological capital 40
  Diaspora's social capital 40
  Policy change in receiving countries 41
  The role of governments in attracting back the diaspora 41
  Sweden and the Sub-Saharan Africa diaspora 42
  Capacity-building for diaspora organisations in Sweden 44

6. Human trafficking 45
  Regional details 45
  Root causes of trafficking 46
  Policy measures 46
  Data on trafficking and legal framework 47
  Public awareness 48

7. Legislative framework governing migration in sub-Saharan Africa 49
  Regional initiatives 49
  ECOWAS free movement of persons 49
  SADC and COMESA 49
  East African Community 50
  Capacity building 50
  Collaboration and cooperation 50

8. Principal actors in migration issues in sub-Saharan Africa 51
  The role of development partners 51
  Other internal and external actors 51
  The Business Sector 51
  Civil Society Organisations 52
  International Financial Institutions 52
  International agencies 52
  Lessons learnt 52

9. Migration and development: challenges and prospects 54
  Trade and migration 54
  Globalisation with a human face 54
  Reducing emigration pressure and providing employment for youths 54
  Research and data on migration 55
  The future outlook 57
  A forum for migration dialogue 57
  Circularity 57

    Public enlightenment 58
    Institutional capacity-building 58

10. Conclusion **59**

References **60**

List of Tables
Table 1: Global flows of migrants' remittances (US$ billion) 2000-06 8
Table 2: International migrants as a percentage of the population, 1960-2005 20
Table 3: Percentage of international migrants by major area or region, 1960-2005 20
Table 4: Growth rate of migrant stock (percentage) 1960-2005 21
Table 5: Female migrants as percentage of all international migrants, 1960-2005 24
Table 6: African immigrants in Sweden by sex in 2004 and 2005 25
Table 7: Nurses and midwives from sub-Saharan Africa on UK register, 1998-2005 26
Table 8: Stock of foreign-born sub-Saharan population in OECD countries, 2002 28
Table 9: Number of expatriates and proportion of highly skilled persons from sub-Saharan African countries living in OECD member countries, 2000-01 30
Table 10: Distribution of sub-Saharan African-born doctors and nurses in various OECD countries, 2000 .. 32
Table 11: Foreign-born sub-Saharan Africans in Sweden, 2006 (selected countries) 42
Table 12: Asylum seekers to Sweden from Burundi, Eritrea and Somalia, 1996-2005 43

List of Figures
Figure 1: Trends in urbanisation – sub-Saharan Africa, 1950-2030 16
Figure 2: Migration routes from sub-Saharan Africa to Europe 23
Figure 3: Sub-Sahara African foreign-born population in OECD countries, 2005 27

Abbreviations and acronyms

ACP	African, Caribbean and Pacific
AU	African Union (formerly OAU)
CeSPI	Centre for International Political Studies (Italy)
COMESA	Common Market of Eastern and Southern Africa
CSO	civil society organisation
CSR	corporate social responsibility
DDNA	Digital Diaspora Network Africa
DRC	Democratic Republic of Congo
EAC	East African Community
ECA	Economic Commission for Africa (UN)
ECOWAS	Economic Community of West African States
EU	European Union
GATS	General Agreement on Trade in Services
GCIM	Global Commission on International Migration
ILO	International Labour Organization
IMF	International Monetary Fund
IOM	International Organization for Migration
MDG	Millennium Development Goals
MIDA	Migration for Development in Africa
NGO	non-governmental organisation
NHS	National Health Service (UK)
OAU	Organisation of African Unity
ODA	Official Development Assistance
RSA	Republic of South Africa
SADC	Southern African Development Community
SANSA	South African Network of Skills Abroad
SID	Society for International Development
SSA	Sub-Saharan Africa
UKNMC	UK Nursing and Midwifery Council
UNECA	United Nations Economic Commission for Africa
UNFPA	United Nations Population Fund
UNICEF	United Nations Children's Fund
WTO	World Trade Organization

1. Why focus on migration?

Introduction

Since the beginning of this century, migration has for a variety of interrelated reasons become prominent in international economic management and trade relations. The fundamental human rights of migrants, especially of the vulnerable – women, children and undocumented migrants – are increasingly critical aspects in the discourse on international migration. The challenge now is to make increasing globalisation work to maximise the opportunities of migration and minimise its drawbacks.

Global economic pressures and tensions are transforming the centre of gravity of economic activities to the emerging market economies and, with it, the skills profile and requirements of the intensive knowledge-based economies (van Agtmael, 2007). The ageing of populations in rich countries is also shaping the direction of economic and demographic management, the need for migrants, and, among other issues, a reshaping of policies on retirement and pension reform. Then, of course, the sticky trade negotiations following the World Trade Organization's (WTO) 'Doha Development Round' have once again brought to the fore the linkages between trade and migration.

Migration – an international agenda

There has been a flurry of events relating to migration and development at international and regional levels in the last five years. These include the report of the Global Commission for International Migration (GCIM) (Geneva, October 2005), the United Nations High-Level Dialogue on Migration and Development (New York, September 2006) and the Global Forum on Migration and Development (Brussels, July 2007). The UN General Assembly informally agreed that the Global Forum be held annually.

The current upsurge of interest in migration can be directly related to the fact that migrants' remittances to *developing* countries increased substantially in 2006: the official estimate of US$206 billion is more than double the level of US$96 billion in 2001 (Table 1). Remittances have thus become a major source of external development finance, overtaking overseas development assistance (Ratha, 2007). Another concern is the adverse effect of the loss of skilled professionals, due in part to the talent-hunting policies of the North (Newland, 2007). Policy makers are now emphasising the potential benefits of international migration for both sending and receiving countries, with a focus on migration management – to optimise the benefits and minimise the adverse effects of migration.

Report of the Global Commission on International Migration

In pursuance of its mandate from the UN Secretary-General to provide a framework for a coherent, comprehensive and global response to the issue of international migration, the GCIM produced a report which posits a migration-development nexus in the context of the three D's – demography, development and democracy – and argues that international migration, especially the contentious issue of the brain drain between North and South, should be placed within this broader context (GCIM, 2005). It also stresses the need to focus on the economic, social and cultural benefits of migration to countries of origin and destination, as well as to the migrants themselves, even in the face of hostility and xenophobia.

TABLE 1: GLOBAL FLOWS OF MIGRANTS' REMITTANCES (US$ BILLION) 2000-06

Region	2000	2001	2002	2003	2004	2005	2006*
East Asia/Pacific	17	20	29	35	39	45	47
Latin America/Caribbean	20	24	28	35	41	48	53
Middle East/North Africa	13	15	16	20	23	24	25
South Asia	17	19	24	31	31	36	41
Sub-Saharan Africa	5	5	5	6	8	9	9
All developing countries	85	96	117	145	165	193	206
World	132	147	170	205	233	262	276

*Estimated
Source: Ratha et al., 2007

The GCIM report argues strongly that migration is an inexorable factor in development and that debate must go further than mere discussion over whether development stimulates or depresses migration. Immigrants bring their energy, determination and enterprise and can galvanise economies through social organisation and the interchange of experience. The major challenge is how to make migration work productively for migrants and their families and for society – in countries of both origin and destination.

The report notes that depressed demographics in the North, together with labour shortages, may slow economic growth and increase the demand for labour, for instance in the healthcare sector. In the South, high population growth has increased the supply of manpower, creating a pool of emigrants with a mix of skills ready to fill vacancies in the North. Nevertheless, global coherence of migration policies, though essential, is still a mirage and a difficult issue in both developed and developing countries. It also briefly addresses the lack of coherence – at national, regional and international levels. There are many stakeholders with divergent interests: the report enjoins civil society and other stakeholders to work more closely with governments, to achieve better coherence in migration policies.

Well managed, migration could result in a win-win-win scenario for migrants and countries of origin and destination. A rational migration management approach must, however, balance the interests and needs of countries of origin, transit and destination as well as the aspirations of the migrants. Migration management is a complex process that goes beyond punitive and control measures. The report emphasised that policy makers need to appreciate that human mobility is an inherent, and desirable, component of the development process and that many prosperous countries and communities have been built on migrant labour in times past. The report also suggests that circular migration can be promoted as a policy measure to enhance the contribution of migrants to the development of destination countries.

The African Union's strategic framework for a policy on migration

In July 2001, the council of ministers of the (then) Organisation of African Unity met in Lusaka and called for a strategic framework for a migration policy in Africa. Given Africa's bright future at the time of independence through the deteriorating economic and political conditions of the late 1970s and 1980s to the perception of a dismal future in the 1990s, many Africans now see migration as a last hope for improving their living standards (Adepoju, 2006e). The aim of the Lusaka summit was to address emerging migratory configurations and ensure the integration of migration and related issues into national and regional agendas for security, stability, development and cooperation. The meeting also agreed to work towards fostering the free movement of people and to strengthening intra- and inter-regional cooperation on migration matters (AUC, 2004). African countries affirmed their commitment to address border problems that threaten peace and security, to strengthen mechanisms for the protection of refugees and to combat trafficking. In addition, they pledged to invest in human resource development to mitigate the brain drain, to promote regional integration and cooperation, as well as economic growth, integration and trade. These commitments reflect the increasing recognition of migration as an engine for regional cooperation and integration and the socioeconomic development of the continent.

The African Union's common position on migration and development

In mid-January 2006, in response to the challenge posed by migration, the eighth ordinary session of the executive council of the African Union (AU) in Khartoum convened an experts' meeting for April that year, to be held in Algiers, to prepare an African common position on migration.

Priority areas covered in Algiers included migration and development; human resources and the brain drain; labour migration; remittances; recognition of the relationships between economic development, trade and migration; increasing the involvement of the African diaspora in development processes; establishing a database of diaspora experts; migration and human rights (ensuring the effective protection of economic, social and cultural rights of migrants, including the right to development); migration and gender (giving particular attention to safeguarding the rights – labour rights and human rights in general – of migrant women in the context of migration management); children and youth (through targeted prevention campaigns, and protection and assistance to victims of trafficking); and migration and health, especially the vulnerability of migrants to HIV/AIDS.

Member states were encouraged, among others things:

- to improve inter-sectoral coordination by establishing a central body to manage migration, using the Strategic Framework for Migration Policies as a guideline;
- to introduce due process measures, including legal frameworks, to fight illegal migration and to punish those guilty of smuggling or trafficking;
- to establish appropriate mechanisms to enable national focal points to exchange information regularly in order to develop a common vision;
- to encourage diaspora input in trade and investment, for the development of countries of origin; and
- to coordinate research on migration and development to provide current and reliable information on migration. (AU, 2006)

The 2006 Euro-African conference on migration and development

The need for Africa-EU cooperation on matters relating to migration, especially between the two regions, assumed centre-stage during a ministerial meeting of 57 African and EU countries in Rabat in July 2006. Recognising that some immigration is necessary, the EU made pledges to help develop African economies, urging African ministers to work together to fight illegal migration in order to facilitate legal migration.

The conference acknowledged that the opportunities and challenges of migration are a reality and form one of the strongest ties between Africa and Europe. According to UN estimates, the number of migrants in the world rose from 100 million in 1980 to 200 million in 2005 and could double again over the next 25 years (UN, 2006a). Africa's migration potential is huge, with half its 800 million people under seventeen years of age and a record-level birth rate differential between Europe and SSA. There are 540 million people in the world living on less than a dollar a day – the majority of them in Africa. For these reasons, the management of population flows is crucial to relations between Africa and Europe today.

This initiative, based on the inseparable links between development and migration, aims to provide an urgent global response to the issue of migration between SSA and Europe, in a partnership among countries of origin, transit and destination. The partnership will work with migrant populations and diasporas in the development, modernisation and innovation of societies of origin, with regard also to structural development at the root of emigration trends, and will work with the countries of origin and transit to build their capacity to manage migratory flows (ILO, 2006).

Among the problems to be tackled are illegal immigration and trafficking in human beings; readmission of illegal immigrants and improvement of legal immigration channels; and implementation of an active policy aimed at integration and fighting exclusion, xenophobia and racism in the destination societies. Finally, the conference saw as imperative the formulation of a 'concrete action plan' to identify the resources needed to implement identified actions quickly and the establishment of a follow-up mechanism to ensure that the actions identified are carried out.

The Joint Africa-EU Declaration on Migration and Development

The ministers of foreign affairs and those responsible for migration and development from Africa and EU member states, EU commissioners and other representatives held a meeting in Sirte, Libya from 22–23 November 2006. The meeting endorsed a joint principle for cooperation and "a partnership between countries of origin, transit and destination to better manage migration in a comprehensive, holistic and balanced manner, and in a spirit of shared responsibility". Participants jointly agreed, among other things, that migration is both a common challenge and opportunity for Africa and the EU and that appropriate responses can best be found together; that well managed, migration can be beneficial to both regions; that the brain drain can have serious consequences for sending countries; and that states must uphold the dignity of all migrants (www.africa-union.org/root/au/conferences). Other decisions included commitment to capacity building to better manage migration and asylum; promotion of regular migration to help meet labour needs in host countries and contribution to the development of countries of origin; cooperation in the control of irregular migration and return in a humane and orderly manner. As a follow-up to the declaration, experts would meet regularly, exchange experiences and information and develop an implementation roadmap for the joint declaration, to be periodically reviewed by the EU-African ministerial conference (www.diplomatie.gouv.fr).

The follow-up meeting to the Rabat Process

On 21 June 2007, a follow-up meeting to the Rabat Process was held in Madrid to advance the Rabat Declaration. The participants agreed on mechanisms to improve coordination, increase visibility of the Process and reinforce the implementation of the action plan. The action plan includes efforts to address the root causes of underdevelopment; the setting up of cooperative programmes and the adoption of measures to facilitate the movement of workers and persons; and promotion of access by regular migrants to education and training. The need to combat irregular migration, smuggling of persons and trafficking in persons, while respecting the fundamental human rights of migrants and refugees, was also of concern.

Among the key decisions was the establishment of a network of contact persons in each participating country. They will be responsible for the internal coordination of the Process and will share information with their counterparts and coordinate the various initiatives to be implemented within the framework of the Process (www.maec.gov.ma/migration/doc). In order to reinforce dialogue within the Rabat Process, countries will organise meetings on migration and development among technical experts, especially on issues dealing with regular migration, the fight against irregular migration and the identification of specific measures and projects to be implemented. A follow-up meeting was scheduled for 2008 to be hosted by France.

The EU-Africa strategic partnership – The Lisbon Summit

As a follow-up to the postponed EU-Africa summit in Lisbon 2003, the second such gathering of African and EU heads of state and government, the summit scheduled for 8–9 December 2007, will sign a Lisbon Declaration. In the preparations and consultations leading up to the summit, the theme, 'Migration, Mobility and Development' featured prominently among the five flagship initiatives. These initiatives will focus on strengthening migration information and management capacities; expanding avenues for circular migration; job creation in the formal economy to redress the employment deficit; promoting the development of migration profiles and efforts to minimise the negative impact of the emigration of highly skilled professionals, especially in healthcare (Commission of the European Communities, 2007).

Three documents are intended to be endorsed at the summit, namely the Joint EU-African Strategy; the Action Plan; and the Lisbon Declaration. The progression from EU Strategy for Africa to a Joint EU-Africa Strategy reflects a remarkable reorientation by the EU from planning for Africa to an Africa-led development agenda (www_europafrica_org.mht). All these and other initiatives discussed above will have to be closely monitored and evaluated.

The UN High-level Dialogue on Migration and Development

A United Nations High-level Dialogue on Migration and Development was held at the General Assembly in New York in September 2006. A culmination of regional and international efforts to increase cooperation on migration and development issues, it was attended by delegates from over 130 countries. The major themes discussed at the four round-table sessions included the effects of international migration on economic and social development; multidimensional aspects of international migration and development, including remittances; respect for and protection of human rights of migrants; preventing and combating trafficking of persons and smuggling of migrants; and capacity building and sharing best practices (Martin et al., 2007).

An important outcome of the dialogue was the platform it provided for states to identify ways to maximise developmental benefits of international migration and promote inter-state consultation. Significantly, it also produced a broad consensus that dialogue should continue in the context of a global forum to permit states to meet regularly to discuss migration matters. The first such forum is described below.

The Global Forum on Migration and Development

The objectives of the first Global Forum on Migration and Development, held in Brussels in July 2007, included confidence- and capacity-building within and across regions; consolidating national, regional and global migration expertise; and contributing to better migration policies in and among states in all regions. Other objectives were raising awareness on the linkage between migration and development by mainstreaming migration in development policies, and better policy coordination at national, regional and international levels.

Key issues flagged for consultation by the Forum included linking migration policies to development policies; maximising the use of remittances; facilitating circular and temporary migration; promoting cooperation and co-development to assist in return and reintegration; the feminisation of migration; the brain drain; global demand for and supply of labour; migrant rights and working conditions; the roles of states, civil society (including diasporas), the private sector and trade unions; human trafficking and migrant smuggling; the protection of children and women; and human and public security.

To ensure concrete outcomes, the meeting limited itself to in-depth examination of only three themes: human capital development and labour mobility (highly-skilled labour migration, temporary labour migration, circular labour migration); remittances and other diaspora resources (formalisation and reduction of transfer costs, increasing the development value of remittances, strategies for enhancing diaspora resources); enhancing institutional and policy coherence and promoting partnerships (the migration and development nexus, enhancing policy coherence and strengthening coordination at the global level) (King Baudouin Foundation, 2007).

Each government nominated a 'focal point' person tasked with ensuring that the right persons attend the Forum and identifying the current priorities of member countries and the way in which these should be addressed. Government officials, policy-makers, international organisations and civil society actors – including the private sector, NGOs, universities, academics, think tanks and diasporas – from about 155 UN member states met for two days, in both plenary and round-table sessions. This was preceded by a Civil Society Organisations' Day, with 210 participants, during which a report was drawn up for presentation to governments the following day. The Forum identified best practices, exchanged experiences, identified obstacles, explored and adopted innovative approaches and fostered cooperation between countries. The next Forum is to be held in the Philippines in 2008.

2. The sub-Saharan African migration scene

Sub-Saharan Africa (SSA) is a region of contradictions: rich in resources, it is the poorest of all regions. Civil wars and political destabilisation have severely eroded the developmental progress of the post-independence decades. In the present trend towards globalisation and economic restructuring, SSA is most disadvantaged. Rather than competing with the rest of the world, it must grapple immediately with more basic and pressing matters: poverty, conflicts and the HIV/AIDS pandemic, all of which severely impact migration dynamics. To place migration within, from and to SSA in its proper perspective, we first outline below the root causes of migration dynamics before clarifying some issues peculiar to the region.

Emigration dynamics: some root causes

The trends and patterns in international migration in sub-Saharan Africa are shaped by many factors: rapid population and labour force growth, unstable politics, escalating ethnic conflict, breakdown of government rooted in precarious democratisation processes, persistent economic decline, retrenchment of public sector workers in response to structural adjustment measures, poverty and – not least – environmental deterioration.

The region's fragile ecosystems, desertification and diminishing arable land have rendered many agricultural workers landless: pastoralists have been compelled to migrate to coastal regions, towns and cities or even to neighbouring countries simply to survive. Abysmally low commodity prices, along with unstable and lowly paid jobs, help explain why migration persists. On top of these are the effects of unfair trade regulations, especially subsidies on cotton by rich countries.

The seasonality and precariousness of the weather has strongly influenced the local ecology. In recent decades, desertification has considerably expanded Africa's arid zones, affecting some 300 million people and now covering almost half the continent. By the late 1980s, there were already some 10 million environmental refugees in Africa, with another 135 million people living on soils deemed vulnerable to desertification, while 80 per cent of all pasture and range lands are threatened by soil erosion. In the last quarter of the twentieth century, land productivity was estimated to have declined by 25 per cent. Sub-Saharan Africa was the only developing region to register a decline in per capita food production during the period 1990–5, and is still doing so (UN, 1996).

Poverty and landlessness are the consequence of a host of interrelated factors – small-sized farms, marginal ecological conditions, depleted soil, low productivity, intense population pressure, lack of access to credit and institutional constraints. Resulting low incomes must be supplemented with earnings from non-farm activities, giving rise directly to out-migration (Findley et al., 1995). Migration often persists even in the face of worsening urban employment conditions because work opportunities, however inadequate, are more abundant than in rural areas. Cities also provide educational opportunities for migrants' children.

Sub-Saharan Africa has been a theatre of internecine warfare for the past three decades or more. Political instability resulting from conflicts is a strong determinant of migration in the region (Crisp, 2006). The political landscape is unpredictable and volatile. Dictatorial regimes often intimidate students, intellectuals and union leaders, spurring the emigration of professionals and others, including refugees. Loss of state capacity, the fluctuating effects of structural adjustment programmes and human insecurity have also prompted migratory movements (Adekanye, 1998).

Macroeconomic adjustment measures and an excruciating external debt have also constrained development efforts in the region. Until the debt burden of 25 of the 29 most heavily-indebted poor countries was eased by the end of 2005, the capacity to mobilise resources for socioeconomic development and to generate employment for the youth was severely constrained by debt-servicing that swallowed nearly two-thirds of export earnings. Other external factors are also relevant, especially the broader international trends – globalisation, regional integration, network formation, political transformation and the entry of multinational corporations in search of cheap labour.

Successive political and economic crises have triggered migration flows to new destinations that have no prior links – historical, political or economic – to the countries of emigration. As the various crises have intensified, migratory outflows have increased in both size and effect. The perception of a dismal economic future has triggered an outflow of emigrants, both male and female. Women – single and married – are now migrating independently in search of secure jobs in rich countries as a survival strategy to augment dwindling family incomes, thus redefining traditional gender roles within families and societies (Adepoju, 2006d).

Sub-Saharan Africa's unemployment rate of 9.8 per cent in 2006 was lower than only that of the Middle East/North Africa region, and it has the highest figure for working poverty. Globally, the number of working poor at the US$1 level declined between 2001 and 2006, but in SSA it increased by 14 million (ILO, 2007).

It is precisely the deficit in decent work that prompts youths to emigrate in desperate quest of a more secure alternative and a future. This they do by undertaking dangerous and uncertain journeys and daredevil ventures to enter Europe in an irregular and undocumented manner. The creation of more productive jobs and decent work locally would hold the promise of arresting the irregular migration of an increasing number of persons, such as these young men and women seeking surreptitious entry into Europe.

Migration or circulation?

Migration in sub-Saharan Africa has been conceptualised as a continuing process of circulation along the origin-migrant-destination continuum (Oucho, 1990). Over the past six decades, concepts such as circulation of labour, circular migration, labour migration, commercial migration, oscillatory migration, target migration and reciprocal migration have pervaded migration literature, reflecting the complexity of migration configurations as perceived through the researchers' lenses. Of all these concepts, 'circulation' seems to encapsulate the essence and specificity of migration dynamics in SSA – non-permanent movements in circuits within and across national boundaries that begin and (must) end at 'home' (Adepoju, 2006c). In some sub-regions, migrants were recruited to work on the understanding that they must return to their countries at the end of their contractual assignment. The mine workers in apartheid-era South Africa are a case in point: migrants recruited from neighbouring states for specified periods had to return home, repeating the process several times if their services were still required (de Fletter, 1986).

Seasonal, short-term and frontier workers regard their own movements as simply an extension across national boundaries of internal movements, seeing them as rural-rural migration. This is especially the case in West Africa. Statistical considerations apart, establishing when a traveller crosses international borders along the extensive frontiers separating homogeneous ethnic agglomerations – for example, the Ewes in Ghana and Togo and the Yorubas in Benin and Nigeria – can be daunting (Adepoju, 2002). It was for such reasons that the term migration and the adjectives prefacing it (target, oscillatory, seasonal, commercial, irregular, undocumented labour) for so long had different connotations among different stakeholders – researchers, policymakers, politicians, government officials and migrants themselves – in different parts of the region and over time.

Internal migration

Intra-rural migration and rural-urban migration are interlinked and dominant patterns of migration in SSA. Landlessness influences the out-migration of farmers from land-deficit to land-surplus areas, as from Lesotho and the Sahel. Fragmented, unproductive landholdings and poor incomes compel farmers to seek wage labour or non-farm activities. The causes and course of intra-rural and rural-urban migrations reflect the effects of contrived economic policies that have systematically marginalised the rural sector. Governments' neglect of the sector fuels unemployment, low productivity, poverty and rural exodus.

Where progressive rural development programmes have been implemented, some return migration has been stimulated and urban to rural return migration, which had been a trickle, has taken hold. In Côte d'Ivoire, Mali, Ghana and Uganda, the removal of marketing boards that formerly paid farmers below market value for their products has enhanced rural incomes and reduced rural out-migration. Another example is Burkinabé migrants in Côte d'Ivoire, who, in the early 1990s, returned home or diverted from urban to rural areas as city life deteriorated and became intolerably expensive, even before the political crisis in the country (Adepoju, 2001). These trends will no doubt be maintained as countries continue to implement policies of structural economic adjustment.

In many parts of SSA, migrants move from one rural area to another – as is the case with seasonal workers from rural Lesotho who work across the border on asparagus farms in South Africa (Adepoju, 2003). In Côte d'Ivoire, Gabon and Ghana, seasonal immigrants do the unglamorous, low-paying manual work on farms and plantations that locals refuse to do, preferring office work instead. In effect, the origin and the destination for these international migrants are no different from that of internal migrants, the decisive factor being the location of the employment opportunities.

Many workers labour in the informal sector with low earnings. Unlike farming, services and factories, the booming oilfields and mines create few jobs. Even South Africa, the region's economic giant, suffers from an unemployment rate of between 25 and 40 per cent. The problem lies, at least in part, with boom-and-bust cycles. Unlike in other world regions, no progress had been made in SSA towards reducing extreme poverty by half by late 2005 in line with Millennium Development Goal (MDG) targets. There has, rather, been a deterioration or reversal in many countries and if prevailing trends continue the target of reducing hunger by half may not be attained even by 2015, except perhaps in Ghana and Mauritius (*The Economist*, 24 June 2006:48).

The preoccupation with the question of why people migrate tends to obscure the other side of the picture, which deals with the question of *non*-mobility, that is, why most people do not migrate from the rural environment or from their countries. The UN and other sources indicate that only about 3 per cent of the world's population are migrants living outside their country of birth (GCIM, 2005; Ratha et al., 2007). Non-mobile persons may be constrained by low levels of material aspiration, or be satisfied with their aspirations under the prevailing opportunity structure, or perhaps have better means of satisfying their aspirations than by migrating. They may also be constrained by institutional and other ties – age, sex, birth rank, lack of education, limited access to information and so on. The end result is that the majority of Africans do not in fact migrate, but those who do migrate are becoming increasingly desperate, exploring diverse destinations through formal and informal entry points, often using the services of bogus traffickers. (Adepoju and Hammar, 1996).

In the face of the rapid growth of population and labour force and sluggish and declining agricultural productivity, the rural exodus to large cities has outpaced urban economies, which are too weak to absorb large numbers of new workers, resulting in further poverty and unemployment. The persistence of city-ward migration, in spite of worsening employment opportunities in the cities, and the continued possibility of earning a living, however meagre, in rural areas is a seemingly paradoxical characteristic of migration in SSA.

FIGURE 1: TRENDS IN URBANISATION – SUB-SAHARAN AFRICA, 1950-2030

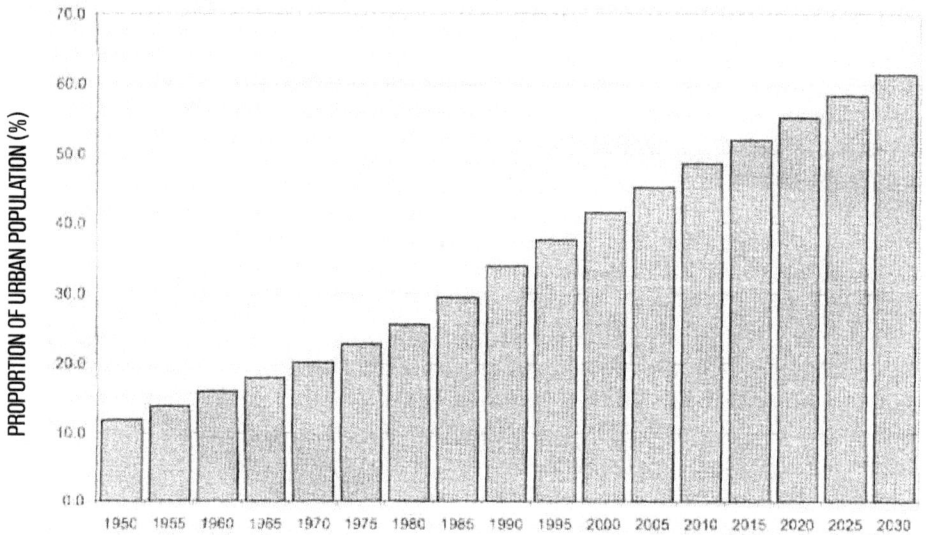

Source: UN, World Population Prospects, 2004

The year 2007 marks a global turning point, with the world's urban population outnumbering the rural population for the first time. SSA should reach that point by 2015, and Asia a little sooner (see Figure 1). Rural-urban migration reflects the neglect of rural areas, especially in terms of inadequate infrastructure, environmental degradation, lack of access to social services and almost no non-agricultural employment. Despite the 'urbanisation of poverty', urban destinations are the choice of a growing number of rural migrants (UN Habitat, 2006) as rural residents continue to migrate to oversized cities with undersized jobs.

Internal migration blends into international migration

Both internal and international migrations result from complex economic and social factors, but the overriding drive is the migrants' search for greater economic well-being. Essentially, people migrate when they are unable to satisfy their aspirations within the structures prevailing in their locality. Development can itself stimulate migration, both internal and international, particularly when improvements in communication, transportation and income raise people's expectations and enhance their desire and ability to migrate (SID, 2002).

International migration can sometimes involve shorter distances, less social heterogeneity and fewer barriers than internal migration. Thus, in SSA, distance, socioeconomic differences and barriers are often more appropriate than national boundaries in classifying migration movements. Indeed, owing to the minuscule geography of some SSA countries (Lesotho, Swaziland, Gambia, Guinea Bissau etc.), short-distance international migration occurs that would elsewhere constitute only internal movement (ECA, 1981). Frontier workers maintain semi-permanent residences on both sides of national frontiers, commuting between home and farm daily.

The distinction between internal and international migration is often blurred by close cultural affinity between homogeneous peoples on opposite sides of national borders – situations in which migrants regard intra-regional migration merely as an extension of internal movement (Adepoju, 1998). As a result of deepening poverty and socioeconomic insecurity, some migration that would otherwise have taken place only internally has been transformed into replacement migration between urban areas, emerging as undocumented emigration across borders to more prosperous countries (Adepoju, 2006c).

Migration patterns in sub-Saharan Africa: some historical trends

SSA is a region characterised by a variety of migration configurations: contract workers, labour migrants, skilled professionals, refugees and displaced persons – in regular and irregular situations – all move within a continuum of internal, intra-regional and international circulation, with most countries serving at a single time as places of origin, of transit and of destination (Adepoju, 2006e). As well as the brain drain from the region, there is a good deal of 'brain circulation' of professionals within it. Some details are now given of historical migration within the four main sub-regions into which sub-Saharan Africa is divided.

West Africa

Intra-regional migration in West Africa is essentially north-south, and the principal countries of emigration include Burkina Faso, Mali, Togo and, in the early 1980s, Ghana. Since the beginning of the twentieth century, workers from Burkina Faso have been attracted to the plantation and construction industries in Côte d'Ivoire and, during the 1950s and 1960s, to cocoa farms in Ghana. Indeed, by 1975, 17 per cent of Burkinabé were living abroad. Contract workers and clandestine migrants from southeast Nigeria worked in plantations of the then Fernando Po and Spanish Guinea (Zachariah and Condé, 1981). About half the immigrants to Senegal came from Guinea Conakry and Guinea Bissau, including refugees who had fled their country for political reasons (Adepoju, 1988a).

Until the 1960s, Ghana's high per capita income made the country the 'gold coast' for thousands of immigrants from Togo, Nigeria and Burkina Faso. Since then, Côte d'Ivoire has replaced it as the principal country of immigration in the sub-region. Côte d'Ivoire's domestic labour force is small and about a quarter of its wage-labour force are foreigners. The country's first post-independent president, ignoring colonial-era borders, encouraged immigrants from Burkina Faso, Mali, Nigeria, Liberia, Senegal and Ghana to do menial jobs in the plantations. By 1995, there were four million immigrants out of a population of 14 million. They were given the right to work, vote, marry local people and own property (Touré, 1998).

By the mid-1970s, Nigeria had become a country of immigration as the oil-led expansion of road and building construction, infrastructure, education and allied sectors attracted workers, both skilled and unskilled, from Ghana, Togo, Benin, Cameroon, Niger and Chad. These workers entered the country through official and unofficial routes and, by 1982, numbered about 2.5 million (Adepoju, 2005b). The deteriorating economic situation in Ghana gave rise to and sustained the exodus of skilled and unskilled persons, both men and women. Academics and professionals, frustrated by deteriorating research and training facilities, readily responded to the demand for their skills and were absorbed into hospitals, government parastatals and schools in Nigeria. Among the sub-regions, Western and Eastern Africa have higher numbers of international migrants, including female international migrants, who increased substantially in number between 1960 and 2000 (Zlotnik, 2003).

In 1969, aliens were expelled from Ghana, with the resulting labour shortages adversely affecting the production of cocoa, the country's major foreign exchange earner. Ghanaians themselves followed the exodus to Nigeria (Anarfi et al., 2003). By 1983, 81 per cent of foreign nationals from the Economic Community of West African States (ECOWAS) legally resident in Nigeria were Ghanaians. Niger came a distant second, at 12 per cent, followed by Togo and Benin (Adepoju, 1988b). That year, two million 'illegal' migrants were expelled from Nigeria, around half of them being Ghanaians. In fact, by the time of the expulsions, 9 per cent of Ghanaians – about 25 per cent of its labour force – had emigrated, mainly to Nigeria, Côte d'Ivoire, Togo, Lesotho, Zimbabwe and even the 'Bantustans' of South Africa, and to Europe (Adepoju, 2005b). This period coincided with the protocol on free movement of persons within the ECOWAS group of states. Ghana and Nigeria have thus experienced 'migration transition' from being receiving to becoming sending countries in recent decades.

Eastern Africa

People migrating between Kenya, Uganda and Tanzania took advantage of a common language, cultural affinity and shared colonial experience, as well as the recently resuscitated East African Economic Community, which offered a unified political and economic space (Oucho, 1998). The sisal, tea and coffee plantations in Tanzania, Kenya's sugar and tea estates and the cotton plantations in Uganda all employed locals as well as foreign labourers from the hinterlands of Rwanda and Burundi, which are densely populated and resource-poor.

Oucho (1995) categorised the countries of the Eastern Africa sub-region into three groups with respect to migration dynamics. Major emigration countries are Eritrea, Ethiopia, Djibouti, Somalia – all in the Horn – as well as Burundi, Rwanda and Mozambique. Immigration countries are Kenya, Tanzania, Malawi and Zimbabwe. And countries of both emigration and immigration are Uganda and Zambia. He adds, however, that a country's net migration status changes over time: for instance Zimbabwe has become a country of emigration in the wake of political crisis and the collapse of the economy, as did Zambia following the slump in the world copper price.

Central Africa

The major countries of immigration in Central Africa are mineral-rich Gabon, Equatorial Guinea and the Democratic Republic of Congo (DRC). The plantation and mining sectors in Gabon and Equatorial Guinea and the palm plantations in Cameroon offer employment opportunities to immigrant labourers from the Central African Republic, Congo and Nigeria, as well as to traders, domestic and service workers from Senegal, Mali, Benin and Togo.

Gabon is a small and rich country, which relies on contract labour and immigrants from other African countries and from Europe – they constitute about a quarter of wage earners. In recent years, thousands of immigrants have entered Gabon from Burundi, Rwanda, DRC and Congo in search of a better life and greater security (Adepoju, 2000). As urban unemployment soared to 20 per cent, a presidential decree was issued in 1991 to safeguard jobs for nationals and 'Gabonise' the labour force, and in September 1994 the government enacted laws requiring foreigners to register and pay residence fees or leave the country by mid-February 1995. After the deadline, about 55,000 foreign nationals were expelled, while 15,000 had legalised their residency (Le Courier, 1997).

Southern Africa

The main migrant labour configuration in Southern Africa has been from nearby countries to meet South Africa's labour requirements. Migrants have been employed in mining, agriculture and domestic services – often filling labour gaps created on (still mostly) white farms by black locals taking up jobs in mining (Ricca, 1989; Adepoju, 1988a). Circular, oscillatory migration was systematically engineered by South African contractual labour laws, which required migrant workers recruited from Botswana, Lesotho, Swaziland, Mozambique and Malawi to leave their families at home, work for two years and then return home for as long as would be economically feasible. This system greatly reduced the social costs normally sustained by receiving countries (Milazi, 1998).

In the 1970s, Lesotho, Malawi and Mozambique were the main suppliers of labour to South Africa. This pattern later changed, with Malawian and Mozambican labour declining during the 1970s – mainly as a result of intensified recruitment from Lesotho (Chilivumbo, 1985). By 1982, Lesotho, at 50 per cent, had become by far the most important supplier of foreign labour to South Africa (de Fletter, 1986).

In recent years, Botswana has become a major country of immigration. A prosperous, stable country with rapid economic growth, it has attracted highly skilled professionals, who are in short supply, from Ghana, Zambia, Uganda, Zimbabwe, Nigeria and Kenya. Most of these people work in the private sector or at the university, taking advantage of the relaxed laws on residence and entry introduced in the early 1990s. However, a new policy of localisation of employment, especially in the education sector, entails replacing expatriates at the university, creating job insecurity for foreigners (Lefko-Everett, 2004; Campbell, 2003).

Trends in the stock of international migration in sub-Saharan Africa

As has been mentioned, the GCIM report points out that in 2005, only about 3 per cent of the world's population were living in countries other than those in which they were born – a proportion that has remained relatively stable since the 1990s (see Table 2). In the African region, however, the percentage of international migrants in the total population has been steadily declining: from 3.2 in 1960, to 2.9 in 1980, and reaching a low 1.9 by 2005. While the Eastern, Central and Southern African sub-regions followed this declining trend, Western Africa started with a lower proportion in the 1960s and, after some fluctuation, overtook the other sub-regions in 1995. It retained that position by 2005, when international migrants constituted 2.9 per cent of its total population (Table 2).

In line with the trend depicted in Table 2, the share of international migrants in Africa as a whole peaked at 14.2 per cent in 1980, up from 12.1 per cent in 1960. Thereafter, the region's share of global migrants declined to 10.6 per cent in 1990 and to 9 per cent in 2005 (Table 3), the lowest of the major regions.

TABLE 2: INTERNATIONAL MIGRANTS AS A PERCENTAGE OF THE POPULATION, 1960-2005

	1960	1965	1970	1975	1980	1985	1990	1995	2000	2005
World	2.50	2.35	2.20	2.13	2.23	2.29	2.93	2.90	2.90	2.95
Developing Regions	2.08	1.85	1.63	1.49	1.57	1.56	1.59	1.42	1.37	1.35
Africa	3.24	2.96	2.74	2.65	2.94	2.61	2.57	2.48	2.03	1.88
Eastern	3.75	3.53	3.15	2.72	3.49	2.70	3.07	2.23	1.78	1.57
Central	4.53	4.88	4.57	3.86	3.60	2.50	2.10	3.19	1.59	1.63
Southern	4.96	4.51	4.05	3.58	3.32	5.24	3.44	2.73	2.43	2.55
Western	2.67	2.59	2.60	3.19	3.31	2.53	2.80	3.25	3.06	2.86

Source: UN, 2007

TABLE 3: PERCENTAGE OF INTERNATIONAL MIGRANTS BY MAJOR AREA OR REGION, 1960-2005

	1960	1965	1970	1975	1980	1985	1990	1995	2000	2005
World	100	100	100	100	100	100	100	100	100	100
Developing Regions	57.2	54.8	52.8	51.1	52.2	51.7	41.7	38.4	37.3	36.7
Africa	12.1	12.0	12.2	12.7	14.2	13.0	10.6	10.9	9.3	9.0
Eastern	4.1	4.2	4.2	3.9	5.1	4.1	3.9	3.0	2.6	2.4
Central	1.9	2.2	2.3	2.1	2.0	1.4	1.0	1.7	0.9	0.9
Southern	1.3	1.3	1.3	1.2	1.1	1.8	0.9	0.8	0.7	0.7
Western	2.8	3.0	3.3	4.3	4.5	3.5	3.2	4.0	4.1	4.0

Source: UN 2007

The fluctuations in the rate of growth of migrant stocks globally are also apparent in the African region. From a less than 1 per cent growth rate in the 1960–65 period, the rate increased consistently till 198590 both globally and in Africa, dipping to a minimum in 1995–2000, and since then the rate has grown only sluggishly (Table 4). Again, West Africa stands out among the sub-regions as having experienced higher than average migrant stock growth rates: at 2.8 per cent this is above the average for other developing countries (1.1 per cent) and indeed is higher even than the global growth rate (2.1 per cent).

TABLE 4: GROWTH RATE OF MIGRANT STOCK (PERCENTAGE) 1960–2005

	1960-1965	1970-1975	1975-1980	1980-1985	1985-1990	1995-2000	2000-2005	1960-2005
World	0.77	1.30	2.69	2.23	6.67	1.36	1.51	2.06
Developing regions	-0.06	0.62	3.12	2.04	2.37	0.77	1.23	1.08
Africa	**0.66**	**2.04**	**4.93**	**0.47**	**2.49**	**-1.68**	**0.68**	**1.39**
Eastern	1.47	-0.01	7.96	-2.13	5.62	-1.92	-0.14	0.84
Central	3.79	-0.72	1.57	-4.38	-0.60	-11.61	3.15	0.46
Southern	0.77	0.18	0.97	11.70	-6.18	-0.55	1.71	0.76
Western	1.75	6.68	3.59	-2.53	4.96	1.43	1.04	2.81

Source: UN 2007

Recent trends in patterns of migration in and from SSA

A unique feature in SSA is that, unlike other regions, international migration includes intra-regional movements by refugees, undocumented migrants and seasonal labour migrants. These migrations, better described as 'circulations', involve more than seven million economically active persons and an unspecified number of undocumented migrants (ILO, 2004. They are largely intra-regional, and account for about 70 per cent of all international migrations (Ratha et al., 2007). Their complex configurations are changing dynamically and are reflected in increasing female migration, the diversification of migration destinations and the transformation of labour flows into commercial migration (Adepoju, 2006f). Coupled with trafficking in human beings and the changing map of refugee flows, these are the key migratory configurations for policy and research in the region.

Diversification of destinations

The unstable economic situation in many SSA cities and the continued weakness of the agricultural sector have drawn more people into circular migration. Many who migrate no longer adhere to classic geographic patterns, but explore a much wider set of destinations than those where traditional seasonal work can be found. New migrations include Senegalese and Malians to Zambia, and more recently to South Africa and the US. Some are now migrating to Libya and Morocco – formerly transit countries (Adepoju, 2006d). This is a response to the now limited opportunities for migration to the traditional labour-receiving countries of the North, where regular labour migration, especially for unskilled and semi-skilled persons, has been virtually closed except for family reunification purposes. The Gulf States have, as a result, become particularly attractive as destinations for highly skilled professionals.

Commercial migration

There is an overall trend away from mere labour migration of unskilled persons towards the commercial migration of entrepreneurs who are self-employed, especially in the informal sector. A large proportion of emigrants from West Africa can be classified as commercial migrants to new regions, especially those from Senegal and Mali (Adepoju, 2004b).

Initially, emigration focused on Zambia, but when its economy collapsed emigration shifted to South Africa following the demise of the apartheid regime. As with labour migration,

Sahelians in West Africa have been moving to Italy, Portugal, Germany, Belgium and Spain, although there they encounter an increasingly hostile reception, with growing xenophobia, apprehension of foreigners and anti-immigrant political mobilisations. A growing number are now crossing the Atlantic to seek greener pastures as petty traders in the United States.

The lure of South Africa and problems of irregular migration

Irregular migration to South Africa intensified in the 1990s as a result of the relative absence of legal mechanisms for entry and work in post-apartheid South Africa. Irregular labour migrants, initially drawn from Lesotho and Mozambique, were soon swamped by Zimbabweans as their country's economy began its collapse. The prospects of a booming economy in a democratic setting opened a floodgate of immigration to South Africa from African and Eastern European countries (Adepoju, 2003). Highly skilled professionals came from Nigeria and Ghana to be employed in universities and in other professions. Traders [?]from Senegal and Mali, joining migrants from the Democratic Republic of Congo, then Zaire, work as street vendors and small traders, invigorating the informal sector through their commercial acumen and by employing locals.

The number of undocumented immigrants in South Africa remains a controversial issue in public policy and public debate. Estimates of undocumented migrants range from 500,000 in the 1990s to the – greatly exaggerated – figure of five to eight million initially flagged by the country's Human Sciences Research Council. Some scholars now argue that an estimate of not more than 1.5 million is more plausible (Oucho and Crush, 2001). These migrants are often accused by the local population of obtaining scarce housing, of taking jobs from locals by working for very low wages, of exploiting South African girls by marrying them merely to obtain residence permits and so on. Many irregular migrants are deported, though those from neighbouring Mozambique and Zimbabwe often find their way back soon after.

Irregular immigrants do not aspire to join unions, for fear of deportation. Many of them must work under constant threat from unscrupulous employers who cheat on their pay packets and threaten to turn their workers over to the authorities. Those who are apprehended and deported are regarded as being shamed and humiliated.

Many irregular migrants do not have the skills that are indispensable to their domestic economy, and, even after several years abroad, may not have acquired such skills. On return home, they may have difficulty in reinserting themselves into the domestic labour market.

The Maghreb – a region of origin, transit and destination

The Maghreb countries, which have traditionally served as a source of migrants to the European Union (EU) countries, especially Spain, France, the Netherlands and Belgium, and to the Gulf States, have also become transit and destination areas. Many SSA youths now enter the Maghreb in the hope of crossing to Europe via southern European outposts.

Since the mid-1990s, increasing migration through and pressure on transit countries of the Maghreb by irregular migrants have intensified border patrolling of the Straits of Gibraltar. This has prompted migrants to cross from more easterly places along the Mediterranean coast (sometimes through the Italian island of Lampedusa) and via the Canary Islands from ports in Senegal and Mauritania (see Figure 2). Between January and September 2004, almost 4,000 irregular migrants were apprehended in Spanish territorial waters while seeking to enter EU territory (European Commission, 2005).

FIGURE 2: MIGRATION ROUTES FROM SUB-SAHARAN AFRICA TO EUROPE

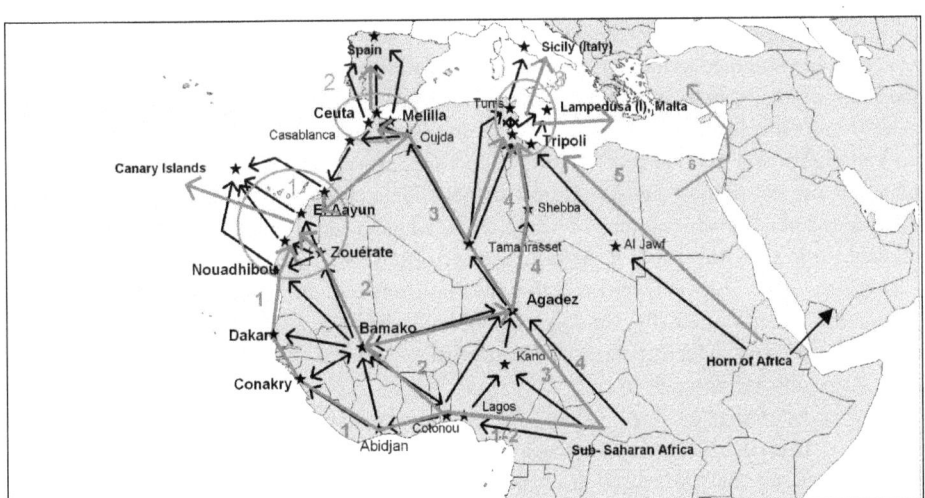

Source: Van Moppes, 2006

Irregular migrants normally combine a variety of modes of transportation – trains, buses, inflatable rafts, rickety fishing boats, speed boats and of course on foot. They manoeuvre their way though dangerous situations, along bush paths, through deserts and inlets, to avoid authorities and check points. The journey is often made in stages and spread over many years, with migrants begging or working for a pittance along the way. These irregular migrants often fall into the hands of bogus agents who swindle them off their hard-earned money with the promise of safe passage by boat to the EU. Having lost all their financial resources – loans, as well as savings – they are caught between the humiliation of repatriation and the trauma of possibly botched attempts at entry into what has become Fortress Europe (Adepoju, 2006b).

This is a great loss of human resource – particularly of youths in the prime of their productive capacity, who waste their lives away in foreign land, struggling endlessly but unsuccessfully to enter European countries clandestinely. Some engage in illicit activities and fall prey to traffickers' rackets in their desperate search for survival. Many now languish in jail. And the numbers simply keep increasing, attesting to the energy, perseverance and desperation of these migrants.

But perhaps the highest cost of irregular migration is the loss of life itself. Irregular immigrants face double jeopardy: they run the risk of dehydration during the long trek across the Sahara desert and of shipwreck during the sea crossing and many lose their lives (Boubakri, 2004). About 2,000 sub-Saharan Africans are believed to drown in the Mediterranean each year while attempting illegal crossings to Europe. Close to 1,000 may have died in the process between December 2005 and May 2006 (*The Economist*, 13 May 2006:31).

Many irregular migrants who fail to reach Europe settle in Morocco rather than face the humiliation of returning home. They do odd jobs in Casablanca, Tangiers and Rabat simply to survive. Apart from irregular migrants attempting to transit through the Maghreb countries to enter Europe clandestinely, there are several thousand others resident and working in regular situations or studying in tertiary institutions in these countries. Statistics are imprecise as to the number, qualifications, employment status, nationality and duration of residence of regular migrants in, especially, Libya, Morocco and Tunisia. These migrants often face hostility and xenophobia from locals, fuelled by the illegal activities of their compatriots in irregular situations.

Libya has emerged as a major transit country for illegal immigrants to Europe, who cross the Strait of Sicily, thus increasing pressure on the EU's external borders in the Mediterranean. This is due in part to the length of Libya's borders and the free movement of people between Libya and the non-Arab countries. In 1998, Libya's leader announced the formation of a new organisation – the Community of Sahel Sahara States – linking Libya with Sudan and the former French colonies of Chad, Mali, Burkina Faso and Niger, and subsequently joined by other nearby states. Many immigrants from these countries, including 500,000 from Chad, have since been attracted to Libya and now account for one-sixth of that country's population (Adepoju, 2006b). Smuggling people has become a major and lucrative business for cartels in Libya, which specialise in transporting Africans through the Sahara desert and then across the Mediterranean.

The outsourcing the responsibility for policing borders and halting irregular migrants to the EU from Maghreb countries is a strategy that is both unrealistic and unsustainable. Included among these Maghreb countries are states with poor human rights records and they also lack the financial and logistical resources to seal-off their borders against irregular immigrants from other parts of Africa and beyond (Boubakri, 2004).

Increase in independent female migration

The traditional pattern of migration in sub-Saharan Africa – male dominated, long-term, long-distance and autonomous – is increasingly becoming feminised as women migrate independently within and across national borders. Anecdotal evidence reveals a striking increase in the numbers of women – who traditionally remained at home – leaving their spouses behind with the children, who, in a reversal of parental responsibilities, are looked after by their fathers or by other female members of the family. The remittances these women send home are a lifeline for family sustenance. A significant proportion of these women are educated and move independently to fulfil their own economic needs: they are no longer simply joining a husband or other family member (Makinwa-Adebusoye, 1990; Adepoju, 2006a). The improved access by females to education and training opportunities and the expansion of the services sector have enhanced their employability locally and across national borders.

TABLE 5: FEMALE MIGRANTS AS PERCENTAGE OF ALL INTERNATIONAL MIGRANTS, 1960-2005

	1960	1965	1970	1975	1980	1985	1990	1995	2000	2005
World	46.8	47.1	47.2	47.4	47.2	47.2	49.0	49.3	49.7	49.6
Developing regions	45.3	45.6	45.8	45.5	44.8	44.4	44.4	44.7	45.1	44.7
Africa	**42.2**	**42.3**	**42.6**	**43.0**	**44.1**	**44.4**	**45.9**	**46.6**	**47.2**	**47.4**
Eastern	41.9	42.3	43.2	44.3	45.3	45.8	47.3	47.9	47.9	48.3
Central	44.0	44.9	45.5	45.8	45.8	45.9	46.0	46.1	46.2	46.3
Southern	30.1	30.3	30.3	32.8	35.6	36.1	38.7	40.0	41.3	42.4
Western	42.1	42.7	43.0	42.6	43.5	45.4	46.4	47.6	48.8	49.0

Source: UN 2007

As indicated in Table 5, the proportion of females in the total international migration stock increased in all sub-regions of SSA throughout the decades 1960–2005. Indeed, in 1960 the proportion of female international migrants in Africa (42.2 per cent) and in SSA (40.6 per cent) was less than the world average (46.8 per cent), but by 2000 that gap had narrowed considerably and SSA female migrants had overtaken their Asian counterparts (at 47.2 and 43.3 per cent respectively) (see Zlotnik, 2003). Table 6 gives the number of African immigrants in Sweden by sex in 2004 and 2005, with some breakdown according to SSA countries. The data sets show a high representation of females among both immigrants and emigrants for the period 2004 and 2005, with the exception of the Nigerians.

TABLE 6: AFRICAN IMMIGRANTS IN SWEDEN BY SEX IN 2004 AND 2005

	2004				2005			
	Immigrants		Emigrants		Immigrants		Emigrants	
Country	Female	Male	Female	Male	Female	Male	Female	Male
Africa	2,100	2,623	729	944	2,510	3,115	690	923
Burundi	168	153	2	0	278	253	2	0
Eritrea	167	97	10	16	277	277	24	14
Ethiopia	173	188	99	134	177	183	91	127
Nigeria	42	168	12	24	79	303	10	33
Somalia	569	590	312	340	680	675	279	290
Other	981	1 427	294	430	1 019	1 424	284	459

Source: Statistics Sweden, 2006

In many parts of the region, the emergence of migrant females as breadwinners puts pressure on traditional gender roles within families. Increasing female migration may be a reflection of pressure on families – women are migrating as a means of reducing absolute dependence on agriculture. As jobs become harder to secure and as remittances thin out in many parts of Western and Southern Africa, many families increasingly rely on women and their farming activities. As more men migrated from rural areas, smallholder agriculture became increasingly feminised (Mbugua, 1997). Women who are left behind assume new roles as resource managers and decision makers, particularly within the agricultural sector. Women are also taking advantage of the expansion of employment opportunities in the urban formal and informal sectors, and this has encouraged their migration to the towns (Oppong, 1997). Independent female migration to attain economic independence through self-employment or wage income is intensifying, and with it the changes in the roles and status of women.

Improving access to education by females means that educated women now have greater opportunities for employment in the urban formal sector and are increasingly, and more effectively, able to compete and participate in both non-domestic and formal sector activities (UNFPA, 2002). The growing proportion of educated females is also reflected in the accelerated migration of women – especially young women – into urban areas to seek further education and jobs. Empowered economically, women are redefining their roles and asserting their independence within the family and society (UNFPA, 2006).

Globalisation has also introduced new labour market dynamics, including a demand for highly skilled healthcare workers. Professional women – nurses and doctors – have been recruited from Nigeria, Ghana, Kenya, Malawi, Zimbabwe, South Africa and Uganda to work in Britain's National Health Service and in private home care centres (Buchan and Dovlo, 2004). Earlier on, women were recruited to work in Saudi Arabia and Kuwait, often leaving their spouses and children behind at home. For example, since 1990, when about 5,000 female nurses were interviewed in Lagos for job placements in the US and Canada, many more have been migrating, taking advantage of the network of colleagues already established (Adegbola, 1990).

The migration of skilled females has become established in the UK as well, with nurses and midwives admitted through the UK Nursing and Midwifery Council (UKNMC, 2005). Statistics from the UKNMC show that, from a trickle of nurses and midwives recruited from Zimbabwe, Ghana, Zambia, Botswana and Malawi in 1998–99, the number rose sharply with a peak in 2000-01, and continued steadily as a result of changes in recruitment codes till 2004–05. South Africa topped the list for sub-Saharan Africa, with over 2,000 nurses and midwives registered in 2001–02. Nigeria followed with about 500. Overall, the number of nurses and midwives from sub-Saharan Africa rose from about 900 in 1998–99 to about 3,800 in 2001-02. It then declined to 2,500 by 2004/05 (Table 7).

Even without the South African figures, this means that in the UK there are thousands of African women deploying home-grown professional skills (UKNMC, 2005). An unknown number were recruited by private agencies to work in care homes for the elderly. Others migrate with their children to pursue their studies abroad, since the educational system in many African countries has virtually collapsed. All these migrations, and the emergence of transnational families, the stability of unions and spousal separations are among the emerging areas of concern and create new challenges for research, public awareness, advocacy and public policy (UNFPA, 2006).

TABLE 7: NURSES AND MIDWIVES FROM SUB-SAHARAN AFRICA ON UK REGISTER, 1998–2005

Country	1998/99	1999/2000	2000/01	2001/02	2002/03	2003/04	2004/05
South Africa	599	1,460	1,086	2,114	1,368	1,689	933
Nigeria	179	208	347	432	509	511	466
Zimbabwe	52	221	382	473	485	391	311
Ghana	40	74	140	195	251	354	272
Zambia	15	40	88	183	133	169	162
Mauritius	6	15	41	62	59	95	102
Kenya	19	29	50	155	152	146	99
Botswana	4	0	87	100	39	90	91
Malawi	1	15	45	75	57	64	52
Lesotho					20	37	34
Sierra Leone							24
Total	915	2,062	2,266	3,789	3,073	3,546	2,546

Source: UKNMC (2005)

A new developmental approach to migration

In January 2007, the EU immigration commissioner unveiled a pilot project for a new 'guest worker' scheme for Africa that aims to boost local economies, enhance the earnings of potential migrants and (hence) stop – or very significantly reduce – irregular migration. The pilot for this flexible scheme is designed to coordinate job offers in the EU with job seekers in – for a start – Mali. Mali was chosen because it has long experience of co-development cooperation with France, is very poor and generates many emigrants, but is also one of the SSA countries to have made considerable progress in the transition to democratic governance. The pilot project allows workers to develop skills and earn money while filling jobs in areas of labour shortage, such as agriculture, construction and sanitation services (as well as seasonal tourism). The EU promises to assist the economy of African countries, starting with Mali, by helping migrants find jobs in the EU, and, in return, Mali is expected to increase its cooperation in the fight against illegal immigration to the EU and to sign a treaty on the repatriation of illegal immigrants. The scheme, to be funded by the EU late in 2007 or early in 2008, will be followed by similar projects in Senegal and Mauritania. Observers argue that these measures are too little and too late in addressing the acute employment problems and poverty that trigger emigration from these countries.

Although the EU is increasing border patrols against irregular immigration both by land and sea, the current strategy is to offer more avenues for regular migration, thus fighting the mafia networks that organise irregular migration. The scheme is modelled on a project in Spain's southern province, which receives 1,000 temporary agricultural workers from Morocco for six months each year. Spanish and EU operations in Senegal have already been effective in dismantling trafficking networks.

FIGURE 3: SUB-SAHARA AFRICAN FOREIGN-BORN POPULATION IN OECD COUNTRIES, 2005

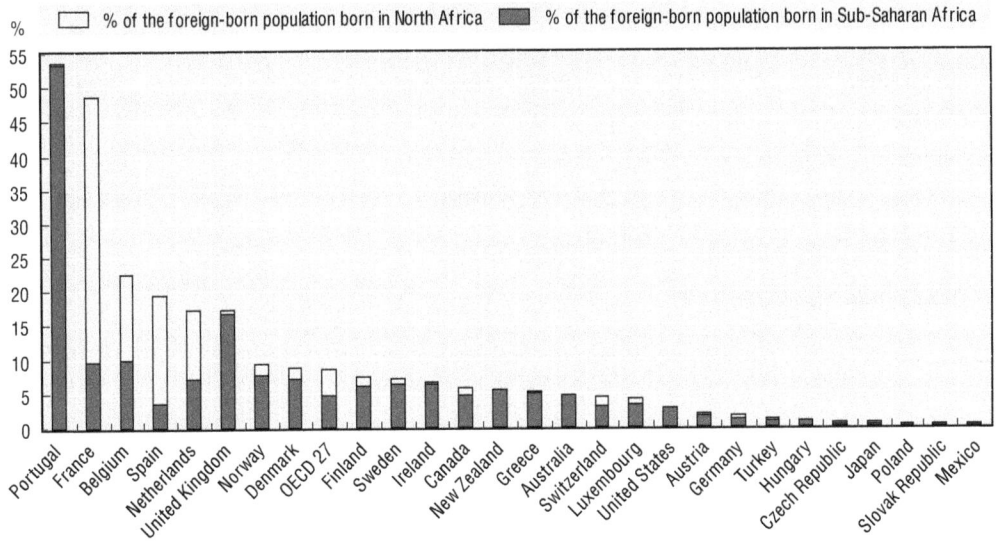

Source: OECD, 2007

Migration to rich countries

There are an estimated nearly four million sub-Saharan Africans resident (but not born) in OECD countries. Major recipient countries in 2002 were the US (929,723), the UK (812,371), France (565,590), Portugal (348,263), Canada (271,095) and Australia (188,928). Others with more than 100,000 sub-Saharan Africans include the Netherlands (116,349) and Belgium (107,716), trailed by Spain (79,263), Sweden (68,077) and Greece (56,859) (see Table 8 and Fig 3). These estimates, which relate to migrants in regular situations, may understate the total stock of immigrants, including an unknown number of undocumented immigrants. West Africans are the predominant Sub-Saharan African immigrants in the US. Of the 929,723 foreign-born SSA population in the US in 2002, 357,360 were from West Africa, including 139,493 Nigerians, with South Africans making up the majority of those from Southern Africa, at 70,275 out of 71,883 (OECD, 2005). These estimates may not include second-generation immigrants and those residents in irregular situations.

TABLE 8: STOCK OF FOREIGN-BORN SUB-SAHARAN POPULATION IN OECD COUNTRIES, 2002

Country	Number of foreign-born stock	Country	Number of foreign-born stock
Australia	188,928	Japan	5,321
Austria	16,374	Luxembourg	4,558
Belgium	107,716	Mexico	952
Canada	271,095	Netherlands	116,349
Czech Rep	47,648	New Zealand	39,078
Denmark	25,355	Norway	25,613
Finland	7,930	Poland	2,221
Former CSFR[1]	1,786	Portugal	348,263
France	565,590	Slovak Rep	354
Germany	124,435	Spain	79,263
Great Britain	812,371	Sweden	68,077
Greece	56,859	Turkey	11,059
Hungary	2,170	USA	929,723
Ireland	25,412	**Total**	**3,884,500**

Source: OECD, 2005

[1] Czech and Slovak Federal Republic (1990-93).

3. Emigration of professionals: causes and consequences

Brain drain: its determinants and magnitude

At independence, sub-Saharan African countries invested heavily in education to train nationals to fill the gaps created by departing colonialists, education being regarded as the main vehicle for rapid development. Within a generation, these countries were able to produce professionals (recently including IT specialists). However, the need for education has expanded faster than the absorptive capacity of these countries' economies. The small private sector and the bloated public sector have absorbed few graduates, resulting in graduate unemployment. Many students sponsored to do postgraduate studies in technology, science and engineering abroad have remained abroad upon completion of their studies (UN, 2003). Emigration of highly qualified professionals from Uganda, Ghana, Zimbabwe, Nigeria and Zambia to South Africa and outside Africa in the 1970s intensified in the 1980s and 1990s, with qualified persons moving to Europe, North America and the oil-rich Middle East (Adepoju, 2005c).

The emigration of highly skilled professionals – including doctors, paramedical personnel, nurses, teachers, engineers, scientists and technologists – from Africa was led by Ugandans and, later, Ghanaians and Nigerians, all of them attracted by relatively higher salaries and better living conditions. Soon after the collapse of Nigeria's oil-led economy in the mid-1980s, many Ghanaian professionals moved from Nigeria in a step-wise pattern to South Africa's then 'homelands', as well as to Swaziland and Lesotho (Adepoju, 2005b). In trickles, brain circulation took place between Ghana, Gambia and Nigeria; Togo and Côte d'Ivoire; Burkina Faso and Senegal and Côte d'Ivoire – all countries with shared colonial legacies.

To cite an example, since the 1990s, Ghanaians have been migrating in ever increasing numbers to rich countries, especially the UK, Germany, the Netherlands and the US. By 1996, Ghana was among the top ten countries sending emigrants to the UK, registering a flow of about 21,500 from 1990 to 2001. More spectacular has been the emigration of skilled personnel: although concrete data may be imprecise, the UN estimates that between 1995 and 2002 about 60.4 per cent of medical officers trained in Ghana during the period emigrated abroad (UN, 2005). Similar percentages obtain for dentists at 27.3 per cent, pharmacists at 43.3 per cent, medical laboratory technologists at 19.5 per cent and nurses/midwives at 19.7 per cent (Anarfi et al., 2003).

Of the estimated four million Africans living in Europe and North America, about 100,000 (2.5 per cent) are professionals. This is, ironically, about the same as the number of expatriate professionals employed by aid agencies as part of the overall SSA aid package over the last two decades – at a cost to the region of about US$4 billion (UN, 2003). Sweden and other development partners should help reverse the emigration trend that denies SSA the use of the abilities of its scarce home-trained skilled manpower.

Highly skilled professionals constitute about a half of Nigerian and Zambian 'expatriates'. Two of every five nationals of Benin, Tanzania, Zimbabwe, Cameroon, Lesotho, Malawi and South Africa working outside their home countries are highly skilled professionals (see Table 9).

Mayer (2001) notes that the number of PhDs listed in the South African Network of *Skills Abroad* was twice as high as in the graduate population at home. About 70,000 people, mostly skilled whites and their families, emigrated from South Africa between 1989 and 1992, and another 166,000 emigrated from 1998 to 2001, sceptical about the prospects under black majority rule and alarmed by the rising crime rate. Most emigrating household heads are engineers, accountants and doctors, those with precisely the skills that South Africa needs to stimulate economic growth. Horowitz and Kaplan (2001) estimate that in spite of the high quality of medical training, doctors' earnings in South Africa were one-fifth doctors' earnings in the US.

Official statistics indicate that 16,000 highly skilled South Africans emigrated between 1994 and 2001, but this may be an under-enumeration as some emigrants retained their names on local professional registers. Other sources indicate that between 70 and 100 doctors emigrate from South Africa every year, and that about 10 per cent of hospital doctors in Canada are South Africans (*The Economist*, 13 August 2005). The figures for South African nurses in the UK have been noted in an earlier section.

It is believed that about one-half of South Africans living in rich countries hold higher-education degrees. At the same time, the number of foreign students from other African countries registered for degrees in South African universities rose from 12,600 in 1994 to 35,000 in 2001 (*The Economist*, 13 August 2005).

TABLE 9: NUMBER OF EXPATRIATES AND PROPORTION OF HIGHLY SKILLED PERSONS FROM SUB-SAHARAN AFRICAN COUNTRIES LIVING IN OECD MEMBER COUNTRIES, 2000–01

Sub-region or country	Total number of expatriates	Percentage of expatriates who are highly skilled
West Africa		
Benin	13,669	43.8
Burkina Faso	6,237	38.4
Cape Verde	83,291	6.2
Côte d'Ivoire	58,843	27.5
Gambia	20,923	16.9
Ghana	150,665	34.0
Guinea	19,684	24.5
Guinea-Bissau	29,449	12.7
Liberia	41,756	33.0
Mali	45,034	12.6
Mauritania	14,813	18.5
Niger	4,948	38.0
Nigeria	247,497	55.1
Senegal	104,715	23.1
Sierra Leone	40,556	33.6
Togo	18,024	36.3
East Africa		
Burundi	10,095	38.6
Djibouti	5,359	29.7
Ethiopia	113,838	31.2
Kenya	197,445	37.4

Malawi	15,024	35.2
Mauritius	86,410	28.0
Mozambique	85,337	26.5
Rwanda	14,832	34.4
Tanzania	70,006	41.0
Uganda	82,232	39.2
Zambia	34,825	49.3
Zimbabwe	77,345	43.3
Central Africa		
Angola	195,674	19.6
Cameroon	57,050	42.3
Central Africa Republic	9,855	32.7
Chad	5,836	42.1
Congo	100,052	36.6
Equatorial Guinea	12,149	22.7
Dem. Rep of Congo	66,488	32.5
Southern Africa		
Botswana	4,298	37.4
Swaziland	2,103	41.7
South Africa	342,947	47.9
Lesotho	995	45.7
Namibia	3,390	45.3

Source: OECD, 2005

Impact of the brain drain

The global migration market allows developed countries to select – unilaterally and freely – which people should be admitted, what skill combinations and income profiles they should have, when they should be admitted and for how long. This process persists without reference to the countries of origin that have invested in human capital in the form of these migrants.

Highly skilled emigrants, though a small proportion of those emigrating, cost their countries in a variety of ways. Sustained emigration poses a critical problem of replacement. An immediate impact is the lack of capacity to undertake cutting-edge research. In addition, emigration creates a huge vacuum of experienced leaders in tertiary institutions for the development and training of younger cohorts. In many countries of the region, students are now being churned out without the requisite rigour in learning (Adepoju, 2007a).

The 'brain drain' is seen most acutely in the departure of health professionals: the exodus of doctors has impacted negatively on the training of new doctors and on the quality of health service delivery. Sixty per cent of doctors trained in Ghana have emigrated to Canada, Britain and the US; thousands of white South African doctors have emigrated to these countries and to Australia; and three-quarters of Zimbabwean doctors have moved to Botswana and South Africa as their country's economy collapses. The driving force is the wide differential in incomes: a trained nurse in Uganda earns $US38 per month and a doctor US$67 per month, while their colleagues in the US could earn about US$3,000 and US$10,000, respectively (UN, 2005; UKNMC, 2005). The acute shortage of doctors has forced the South African government to recruit foreign doctors, especially from Zimbabwe and Cuba, the latter to work mainly in the under-served rural areas (Adepoju, 2003). In the US, the Department of Health and Human Sciences has projected a shortfall of about 270,000 full-time registered nurses by 2010 and 800,000 by 2020 (Clearfield and Batalova, 2007). Already in 2005, 15 per cent of all healthcare workers in the US were foreign-born.

The impact of the brain drain from SSA is captured in a UN report that estimates 'over the next decade Africa will need to train an additional 1 million healthcare professionals. The leaders must find ways to retain more of the doctors, nurses, pharmacists and laboratory technicians it currently produces' (UN 2005:18). Blaming rich countries for contributing to the crisis by creating a 'fatal flow' of health professions from the region, the report points out that there are more Malawian doctors practising in Manchester, UK, than in Malawi itself, while 550 of the 600 Zambian doctors trained between 1978 and 1999 have emigrated (UN, 2005:18). The International Organisation for Migration (IOM, 2003) reports in similar vein that more Ethiopian doctors are practising in Chicago than in Ethiopia. More than half of the nurses and doctors have emigrated from Malawi, and another quarter of the remaining health workers are thought to be infected with HIV/AIDS. Half of Zimbabwe's social health workers have relocated abroad since 2001.

TABLE 10: DISTRIBUTION OF FOREIGN-BORN DOCTORS AND NURSES FROM SUB-SAHARAN AFRICA IN VARIOUS OECD COUNTRIES, 2000

Country/region	Doctors	Nurses
Australia	0.7	0.4
Canada	12.1	3.9
Denmark	2.8	4.4
Finland	2.6	3.2
France	11.3	15.8
Great Britain	16.9	25.4
Greece	4.8	1.8
Hungary	2.9	0.1
Ireland	6.5	3.6
Luxemburg	5.6	4.0
New Zealand	15.9	7.7
Portugal	61.4	57.6
Country/region	Doctors	Nurses
Spain	1.7	3.1
Sweden	2.9	2.6
USA	4.6	6.1
OECD	7.8	8.4

Source: OECD, 2007:208-9

Overall, as indicated in Table 10, 7.8 per cent of doctors and 8.4 per cent of nurses practising in OECD countries are SSA-born. Indeed, a quarter of the nurses in the UK and 17 per cent of doctors are of SSA origin. In France, Canada and New Zealand, the corresponding percentages of doctors of SSA origin are 11, 12 and 16 respectively. Portugal stands out, with well over half its medical professionals being of SSA origin, mostly from former colonies.

Sub-Saharan African countries thus pay the price of producing human capital for use by richer countries, while their own development goals are severely constrained by the outflow of scarce skilled manpower (UN, 2006b). This has been occurring even as the local healthcare situation is worsening, especially in respect of HIV/AIDS infection, and the previously declining rate of under-5 mortality has reversed in many parts of the region (Adepoju, 2005c).

Rich countries have been luring specialists from Africa and other poor regions in a recent policy of talent hunting or 'battle for brains'. Germany's 2005 Green Card scheme creates opportunities for admitting academics and specialists in the technology sector by offering them permanent residence. Family members can work without restriction and are not subject to 'integration requirements'. France's new immigration and integration bill aims to secure more elective immigration for work, study and research, with a focus on migrants who could contribute to France's economic development (*The Economist*, 6 May 2006:29). Britain's points system, adopted in 2006, offers highly skilled migrants a residence permit for up to five years, allowing job changes without further verification. At the end of their studies, foreign students may work for a year in England (or two years in Scotland). In the Netherlands, the government's 2004 'inviting policy' uses a system based on personal talents, age, education and work experience, which has simplified the admission of highly qualified professionals from developing countries (Netherlands Government, 2006).

African leaders argue that the importation of skilled manpower from poorer to rich countries is but a short-term solution to the problem of acute skills shortage: in the long-term the solution lies in improving training and educational opportunities in the North. Given favourable working conditions, skilled professionals, both men and women, would prefer to remain in their home countries and those in diaspora would opt to return home to contribute to local development (Adepoju, 2007a).

Measures by donor communities to counter negative effects

Criticism from Nelson Mandela prompted the UK ministry of health to issue guidelines to all NHS employers in November 1999 to refrain from active recruiting, especially from South Africa and the Caribbean (Buchan and Dovlo, 2004). The UK was the first country to develop such guidelines and the first (in 2001) to develop a code of practice for employers. A memorandum of understanding, signed by the UK and South Africa in October 2003, included clauses for active cooperation in monitoring recruitment agencies accredited by the UK government (RSA, 2004; 2005) and was based on the 2003 International Code of Practice on the Ethical Recruitment of Health Workers (see Commonwealth Secretariat, 2003).

The problem with ethical codes lies in their enforcement: only 59 per cent of UK private sector recruitment agencies signed the 2001 code. Non-NHS employers and recruitment agencies continued to recruit from South Africa and increased recruitment from Nigeria, Ghana and Zimbabwe (Buchan, 2002; Bach, 2003). Migration policies can no longer be handled bilaterally: to be effective, ethical recruitment codes have to be at least regional in scope and/or have a global remit, and require international monitoring.

It is important then for Sweden – and other destination countries – in a spirit of co-responsibility to help foster local development, reduce poverty and create domestic employment in countries of origin. The rich countries should support dialogue and consultation to discuss common approaches to migration concerns. Cooperation in the management of skilled migration should include adoption of flexible residential rules to give skilled professionals the opportunity for virtual relocation without losing residence rights (Adepoju, 2007b). Receiving countries can also help cover the investments in training and education in countries of origin by instituting a 'brain tax'. The primary response of governments and donors must be to support the human resource base of developing countries and their health systems in particular. Compensation for the brain drain can take the form of supporting projects that involve professionals going back to their countries of origin for short periods to work in special health and education programmes, thus addressing the haemorrhaging of poor countries' scarce skilled manpower resources.

Above all, it is essential for countries such as Sweden to support the initiatives of sending countries to strengthen linkages with their diaspora communities overseas; to provide infrastructural facilities and opportunities for overseas nationals to invest in their home countries; and to promote the active involvement of local communities in developing and implementing reintegration programmes for returnees by fostering possibilities for investment and entrepreneurship.

Brain circulation and skills circulation

In sub-Saharan Africa, brain drain is gradually being transformed into brain circulation, especially to Côte d'Ivoire, Gabon, Botswana, Namibia and South Africa. As political and economic crises continue to affect traditional countries of immigration, highly skilled professionals have found politically transformed post-apartheid South Africa and the booming economy of Botswana attractive alternatives to Europe, North America and the Gulf States (Adepoju, 2006e). Both brain drain and brain circulation originate largely in those countries that have invested heavily in human resources development: Ghana, Uganda, Nigeria and Kenya. Their patterns of internal and intra-regional migration are similar, with highly educated men and women, who were employed in their home countries in urban areas and in sectors where skills are short (tertiary institutions, industries and parastatals) taking up similar posts in the destination countries.

New migrants to South Africa are mostly skilled professionals – professors, doctors, lawyers, nurses and engineers – unlike the traditional immigrants from Lesotho, Swaziland, Botswana, Malawi and Mozambique, who were mostly unskilled mine workers and farm labourers. But South Africa is no longer only a recipient but a sender, perhaps also a transit, country, exporting skilled migrants to Europe, North America and Australia (Adepoju, 2003). There are about 300,000 unfilled posts in South Africa requiring skills that nationals do not possess – in a situation of about 40 per cent unemployment, with skilled white professionals emigrating to what they see as safer, richer economies.

The thousands who emigrated from South Africa just before and soon after 1994 were mostly skilled whites and their families, sceptical of the prospects of black majority rule. Networks built with previous emigrés facilitated the emigration of young professionals in and around 1994. Emigrants attracted by higher earnings in developed countries were, and are, mostly engineers, accountants and doctors, forcing the government to recruit foreign doctors (Adepoju, 2003). Dislodged white farmers from Zimbabwe are moving to neighbouring countries such as Zambia, Mozambique and Malawi, and a few to Angola. Concerned at possibility of Zimbabwe-style land appropriation for indigenes, some white South African farmers are also emigrating – to the farmlands of the DRC, the Republic of Congo, Mozambique, Nigeria and Zambia. Both trends constitute a rural-rural migratory pattern. To increase domestic food production, the Congo and Mozambique have granted immigrants access to state-owned farmland. Some South African entrepreneurs are migrating to the gold fields in Chad, Mali and Ghana (Adepoju, 2000).

Botswana has evolved from a migrant-sending to a migrant-receiving country, attracting skilled professionals. Fuelled by political stability, a fast-growing economy, prudent economic management and a small largely unskilled local labour force, most migrants to Botswana are highly skilled professionals in industry, university and the private sector (Adepoju, 2003). The number of non-nationals legally resident in Botswana tripled from 10,860 in 1971 to 29,560 in 1991 and had reached 60,720 by 2001 (Lefko-Everett, 2004).

4. The characteristics and roles of remittances in sub-Saharan Africa

The sheer volume of remittances has kindled optimism about their positive contribution to development in home countries and the role of the diaspora in that development. In 2006, estimated global inflows of international migrant remittances through official channels was US$276 billion, a figure set to reach US$300 billion in 2007. Developing countries recorded US$193 billion in remittances in 2005 (Table 1). India, Mexico, China and the Philippines were the top four countries receiving remittances in 2006. In 2005 Filipinos in the diaspora remitted about US$10.7 billion through formal channels, an increase of 25 per cent over the US$8.6 billion recorded in 2004, and Indians transferred US$24.6 billion, up from US$23.5 billion in 2005 (see, among others, Chishti, 2007; Ratha, 2007).

Migrant remittances are a major source of income in many sub-Saharan African countries. Remittance values have risen steeply in Burkina Faso, Ghana, Egypt, Eritrea, Lesotho, Mali, Nigeria, Senegal, Somalia, Burkina Faso and Cape Verde and now parallel export earnings or ODA (Azam and Gubert, 2005). In Lesotho in 2005, estimated remittances represented 22.5 per cent of GDP (Ratha, 2007). Even then, though, SSA remained the region with the lowest inflow of migrants' remittances (see Table 1).

Use of remittances

Remittances help sustain and enhance the lives of poor home communities and meet their many needs. These include daily needs (consumption, clothes, rent), consumer durables (such as radio, TV, fridge), healthcare (medication and hospitalisation), savings and investments and housing (purchase, refurbishment). Remittances also pay for basic education for siblings (school fees, textbooks, uniforms) and for improvements in agriculture, such as irrigation schemes, as well as for improving basic infrastructural facilities through hometown associations (Orozco, 2007). Some migrants use their remittances to invest in real estate or to set up small enterprises in preparation for their return (IMP, 2003). Alleviating the poverty of poor households also has multiplier effects, generating jobs and incomes within local communities and within the economy of the country as a whole.

Some experts have suggested that remittances should be taxed by recipient countries, or that they should be linked to ODA. But as the GCIM report (GCIM, 2005) emphasised, they are private money, earned by hard work, and migrants should be free to spend them to fulfil their own needs and those of their families. In fact there is a need to reduce transaction charges and transfer costs and the risks of transfer – as is discussed below.

Migrants also foster 'social' remittances by way of ideas and social capital. These can affect attitudes towards human rights, women's rights, the value given to girls' education and to women's employment.

Remittances: micro-meso-macro levels

Remitting money formally – for example by moneygram – is an expensive business. Irregular migrants must therefore use traditional couriers to avoid being apprehended and deported. The discourse in sub-Saharan Africa now centres on how to make remittances work productively for poor recipients, communities and countries and on how to reduce transaction costs, minimise transfer risks and develop the domestic environment for investment. In Kenya, families receiving remittances were able to amass greater productive capital than those not receiving such remittances. In rural areas of Burkina Faso, remittances reportedly reduced the population living under the poverty line by 7.2 per cent (Ratha et al., 2007).

For a long time, the view prevailed that remittances were used for conspicuous consumption and that they fuelled inflation and aggravated inequalities. However, migration in the region is essentially, and increasingly, a survival strategy. Families must decide who should migrate, where they should migrate and for how long. The emigration of poor people is sometimes funded through cooperative assistance or outright loans, and remittances are used to repay such loans. Remittances also ensure an inter-generational link between migrants and home-place – at family, community and national levels (Adepoju, 2006a).

As has been mentioned, at the community level remittances to hometown associations assist in improving education, health and infrastructural facilities and recreation centres – responsibilities of municipal authorities – thus benefiting all households, not only those of migrants. At the national level, migrant remittances constitute an important source of foreign exchange, for example for Burkina Faso, Senegal, Somalia, Lesotho and Eritrea, whose nationals working abroad remit huge sums of money home, thus easing credit constraints.

As well as foreign remittances there are also those in cash and kind flowing from urban residents to their rural origins. These are, however, largely unrecorded (Sander and Maimbo, 2003). The demonstration effect of these remittances and frugal expenditures by visiting migrants often prompt the emigration of youths to urban areas and, when they fail to find viable employment opportunities there, to richer countries, in search of the illusory greener pastures.

A caveat remains: we need to investigate systematically the behaviour of second-and third-generation immigrants, who are less likely to send remittances or to retire 'home'.

Remittance policy measures

Policy research is needed on how best to make remittances work productively for poor recipients – individuals, households and communities – without increasing dependence, and on how to reduce the reliance of rural dwellers, who make up the majority of sub-Saharan Africans, on remittances.

Transaction costs and incentives

High transaction costs and, for 'irregulars', the risk of deportation discourage many migrants from using official channels to remit money. Instead they opt for informal, trust-based human courier systems and networks of traders. This avoids exchange rate fluctuations and overcomes the bottleneck resulting from poor accessibility to remote rural areas where many recipients live, and the perennial problems of identification and identity fraud.

Remittances are critical to the economy of countries that send migrants – they are the second most important source of foreign exchange after exports. For example, in Senegal in 2004 the estimated 2.5 million emigrants sent about US$618 million home: this is equivalent to a third of the national budget, excluding informal transactions. The Central Bank of Ghana estimated that US$1.2 billion in remittances flowed into the country in 2004 (Mutume, 2005; Bump, 2006). Cape Verde migrants live in 25 countries across the globe and their remittances are indispensable for the sustenance of households back home (Carling, 2002). Malians resident in France remit US$50 million, about the same amount as France's annual aid to Mali, and have built schools and health clinics, paid for road repairs and invested in small business enterprises in their home communities. The governments of Ghana, Senegal, Mali and Kenya promote remittance investment and use their embassies to disseminate information on domestic investment opportunities.

The rapid upsurge in the formal remittances of Ghanaians in the diaspora since 2003 is in part a response to their government's new favourable (tax and related) incentive-based policy environment. These new funds have been invested in real estate or used to set up micro-enterprises and build clinics and schools. A similar situation obtains in Senegal, where hospitals have also been funded. When the Ugandan government implemented measures permitting residents to open foreign currency accounts locally, private transfers to the country increased from US$80 million in 1991 to US$415 million in 1996. In 2002, about 28 per cent of deposits were into foreign accounts (Sander and Maimbo, 2003).

All stakeholders – governments, financial institutions, regulatory agencies, hometown associations, migrant communities, researchers and development institutions – should work to explore opportunities and minimise obstacles for sending remittances. They should lobby for low-cost transfer services and less stringent regulations to increase the micro-meso-macro level productive use of these funds. In a welcome development, some banks in France are now offering transfer schemes to Senegal, Mali and Côte d'Ivoire with significantly lower fees than private money-courier services, though this does not address the problems of possible deportation faced by irregular immigrants to that country.

Policies aimed at improving competition and reducing cost and informality, promoting tax relief for remitters, as well as alternative payment instruments – including the use of debit cards and mobile phones – should be explored and pursued, as should other policies that reach out to the diaspora and engage governments in fostering an enabling environment for investment (Orozco, 2007). Tax relief on remittances could be pooled in a special fund that could be used for development.

Remittances and development
Can remittances drive the development of sending countries? While development partners, international financial institutions (especially the World Bank and the IMF), researchers and policy makers are showcasing the huge remittance flows, which are essentially private transfers (Ghosh, 2006; Azam and Gubert, 2005, Ratha, 2007), we should not be tempted – as seems to be the discourse in some quarters – to identify remittances with development funding, or to see them as a substitute for such aid.
In reality, few governments have unfettered access to remittances, since these are mostly person-to-person private transfers generally sent through informal networks or directly to household members. The exception is Lesotho, which entered into a bilateral agreement with South Africa in the 1970s to ensure that its nationals working in South African mines remitted 60 per cent of their earnings through the bank in a compulsory 'deferred payment scheme' (Adepoju, 2003).
We should also not overlook the fact that emigrants suffer isolation, endure unsociable working hours and are alienated from their partners and their children. This last often results in marital and family disruptions, especially in the case of independent female migrants and those with transnational families. Many migrants have difficulty in finding housing, fuelling bitterness and anger. Many endure job dissatisfaction as a result of under-use of their skills

and face long-term skills loss, which can create problems for their reinsertion into domestic job markets when they return home. Our enthusiasm for remittances, their volume and usefulness, should not blind us to the need to focus on the various levels of trauma migrants may face at their destination and when they return home. We must also note that second- and third-generation migrants and migrants who have been united with their families may not feel a pressing need to send remittances home.

5. The role of the diaspora in country-of-origin development

The migrant-diaspora-return continuum and its linkages are both strong and pervasive in the region. During their sojourn abroad, migrants maintain contact by sending money home and by visiting when possible (Koser, 2003). Sub-Saharan African migrants, including those residing in developed countries, do not intend to stay there indefinitely and actualise their vision of returning home permanently by keeping their wives and children in their countries of origin: these resident families in effect become 'hostages' to guarantee the migrants' return. Migrants in SSA thus lead dual lives, socially and economically. In Lesotho, for example, women stay behind to till the family farm to retain ownership (Adepoju, 1998).

The families of migrants maintain their extended structure despite losses to the workforce through migration and maximise economic returns simultaneously from home and destination areas. In Senegal, Mali and Burkina Faso, families finance migrants' journeys through loans from family members, cooperatives and religious brotherhoods. These loans must be recouped soon after arrival, which is why some immigrants pursue their enterprises aggressively and often successfully at their destination, to the envy of the local population. By retaining close and supportive relations with the migrant, the family ensures that it will share in whatever benefits the migrant attains by his or her mobility (Findley, 1997).

Diaspora's economic and technological capital

The diaspora can promote the flow of trade, capital and technology back to countries of origin (Block, 2005). Migrants can acquire skills, save capital to invest in ventures back home and boost local productivity by introducing modern techniques in farming or local enterprises – as has happened in Mali and Senegal.

In 2004, a group of Nigerian doctors in the US began establishing state-of-the-art hospitals in Nigeria to cater for locals who would otherwise have had to seek treatment abroad at exorbitant cost (Adepoju, 2004b). Another example is the MIDA-Ghana project, strengthening the Ghanaian health sector by involving Ghanaian health professionals in the Netherlands and the UK (African Diaspora Summit, 2003). About 60 per cent of Ghanaian doctors now practise in rich countries, and, as noted earlier, Malawi has more doctors practising in Manchester, UK than at home (Adepoju, 2006e). Beninoise migrants' associations in France encourage migrant doctors to engage in voluntary work in Benin for one month a year. Such initiatives are worth promoting – indeed worth extending to other professions.

Diaspora's social capital

Sub-Saharan African transnational communities rarely sever ties with home, their aim being to return home eventually, even if only in retirement. They are active in political advocacy – especially in Nigeria and Ghana – and in charity and cultural exchange. Their associations help new arrivals adapt and insert themselves into labour markets and they mobilise members' capital for investment and for community development projects 'at home'.

These migrants are sources of financial flow and technology transfer and serve as a bridge into the home country for international ideas. Members of the Ghanaian diaspora in the UK are actively involved in modernising the democratic process at home, for example gaining a concession to enable members to vote in national elections. Nigerian diaspora organisations conducted skills audits in Europe, the Americas and other African countries where there are large concentrations of Nigerians. An annual summit of the Nigerian diaspora is held in Abuja to transfer expertise in technology, in agro-business, IT and so on. Nigerian and Ghanaian professionals have returned to participate in the new political dispensation, serving in key political offices in commerce and industry.

Policy change in receiving countries

Building networks between diaspora scientists and their colleagues at home enables these professionals to contribute to the development of home countries without residential relocation. However, as has been mentioned, the tough immigration policies of rich countries deny many scientists the flexibility to relocate without losing residence rights. A change in such policies could pay dividends in the long run, even to receiving countries (IEmed 2004).

The role of governments in attracting back the diaspora

A major challenge facing sub-Saharan Africa is how to attract back skilled emigrants for national development – an aim that should be encouraged and supported by development partners and rich countries. Leaders in Kenya, Nigeria, Senegal, Ghana and Uganda are exploring various strategies. They have held meetings with their nationals in the diaspora with offers of incentives to return. But they must also address the 'push' factors that spurred the brain drain in the first place and provide returnees with places to work in environments conducive to productivity, and with due reward for their efforts.

Too often, skills that migrants have acquired could be productively used back home but do not match available job opportunities. We need more research on lessons learnt from the Return and Reintegration of Qualified Nationals in Africa project of the International Organization for Migration (IOM, 2004), that facilitated the return, retention and reintegration of about 2,000 professionals for country-of-origin development.

Some foreign international corporations in Europe have launched programmes to recruit Africans in the diaspora to work in their firms in Africa. The Transfer of Knowledge through Expatriate Nationals project aims to persuade professionals established abroad to return, at least temporarily, and thus contribute to national development. In 2002, the UNDP paid for 133 Malians to return as consultants to teach and do research in local universities (MPI, 2002).

Initiatives aimed at attracting back skilled African professionals and utilising their expertise include the Digital Diaspora Network Africa (DDNA) launched in mid-2002, the South African Network of Skills Abroad (SANSA), the Research and Development Forum for Science-led Development in Africa and the African Foundation for Research and Development (Mayer, 2001; UN, 2003). DDNA focuses on reversing the loss of economists, engineers, medical doctors, scientists, information technologists and other highly skilled professionals in short supply in Africa. Both SANSA and the Homecoming Revolution target South African expatriate graduates in medicine, education and engineering, especially in Canada, Australia, the UK and the US, the latter initiative offering practical help as well as advice. Such initiatives should be supported by the rich countries that are currently depleting the region of its skilled professionals and by development partners.

In the same vein, the Homecoming Summit held in Accra in 2001 encouraged Ghanaian businessmen and women in the diaspora to return, with incentives including favourable local investment opportunities and tax-relief (Ghanaian Government, 2001). The Ghana

Dual Citizenship Regulation Act of 2002 allowed Ghanaians to keep their citizenship after obtaining the citizenship of another country. The Non-Resident Ghanaians Secretariat, set up in May 2003, promotes links with Ghanaians abroad and encourages them to return. In Senegal, the Ministry of Foreign Affairs and Senegalese Abroad was restructured in 1993 to enhance the welfare of nationals abroad, including their repatriation and rehabilitation. Emigrants are thus encouraged to be actively involved in the socioeconomic development of Senegal. Like many other SSA countries, Mali has created a ministerial-level post to conduct public relations visits to help receiving countries appreciate the peculiar situation prompting the emigration of Malians, and consular positions have been expanded in the major receiving countries to deal with the return of nationals.

Sweden and the Sub-Saharan Africa diaspora

The first non-European refugees to Sweden were about 1,000 Asians expelled from Uganda in 1972 (Westin, 2006). During the era of family unification (1972–89), the only significant numbers entering the country from SSA were refugees from Ethiopia and Somalia. The numbers from these countries and from the Great Lakes region and parts of West Africa reached 26,500 in 2004, as established refugees sponsored members of their families who were accepted for permanent residence in Sweden (Westin, 2006). By 2005, only 70,000 of the 1.1 million foreign-born people in Sweden (of a total population of 9 million) were of sub-Saharan Africa origin (Muenz, 2006). Of the estimated nearly 4 million SSA foreign-born people in OECD countries in 2002, only about 68,000 were living in Sweden (see Table 8). They are mostly asylum-seekers, and, as indicated in Table 11, are drawn mostly from Ethiopia, Somalia, Burundi, Eritrea and to a lesser extent, Nigeria.

TABLE 11: FOREIGN-BORN SUB-SAHARAN AFRICANS IN SWEDEN, 2006 (SELECTED COUNTRIES)

Country	Foreign-born population	Country	Foreign-born population
Ethiopia	9,251	Sierra Leone	96
Somalia	7,194	Congo	86
Uganda	1,804	Comoros	41
Gambia	1,476	Rwanda	39
Ghana	631	Mali	33
Burundi	578	Djibouti	29
Tanzania	547	Namibia	29
Nigeria	403	Malawi	28
Côte d'Ivoire	176	Lesotho	19
Togo	167	Benin	17
Zambia	155	Swaziland	12
Senegal	150	Chad	11
Zimbabwe	138	**Total**	**23 234**
Mozambique	124		

Source: OECD website

TABLE 12: ASYLUM SEEKERS IN SWEDEN FROM BURUNDI, ERITREA AND SOMALIA, 1996–2005

Origin	1996	1997	1998	1999	2000
Burundi	7	17	1	3	11
Eritrea	33	21	27	73	127
Somalia	434	364	228	289	260
All countries	5,753	9,662	12,844	11,231	16,303

Origin	2001	2002	2003	2004	2005
Burundi	61	135	237	393	427
Eritrea	151	266	641	395	425
Somalia	125	1107	3069	905	422
All countries	23,515	33,016	31,348	23,161	17,530

Source: OECD, 2007:325

Table 12 shows the flow of asylum seekers, mostly from Burundi, Eritrea and Somalia, from 1996 to 2005. The stream has been consistently dominated by citizens of Somalia, a failed state that is still embroiled in political crisis. Along with Ethiopians, these constitute the majority of SSA-born residents in Sweden. Other smaller groups are from Uganda, Gambia, Tanzania and Nigeria.

Sweden is receiving immigrants in record numbers, but few voices are calling for closing the borders. In many European countries, anti-immigration sentiment and concerns about the failing integration of minorities are growing. In Sweden, in contrast, attitudes remain remarkably positive, and the new centre-right government says it has no immediate plans to stem the tide of newcomers. As the migration minister has said, 'A high level [of immigration] is not a problem per se. The problem is to get people to work' (Olson et al., 2006).

An EU Eurobarometer survey at the end of 2006 showed Swedes had the most positive attitudes towards immigrants, with 77 per cent saying they contribute a lot to society, compared to 30 per cent in Germany and an EU average of 40 per cent. The Swedish national statistics office projected that immigration would reach its highest level in 2006, led by Iraqis fleeing violence and Poles looking for work. An estimated 81,000 foreign nationals moved to Sweden in 2006, up 58 per cent from 2005, due mainly to a temporary law that allowed thousands of asylum-seekers to stay in Sweden even though they had previously been denied residency permits. Sweden, where about 12 per cent of residents are foreign-born, kept its borders relatively open and is one of only three EU countries to allow unrestricted access to workers from the ten new member states that joined in 2004, unlike Denmark and the Netherlands, hitherto known as among the most welcoming nations to immigrants. Conservatives say that the country will soon be forced to cut immigration sharply (Olson, et al., 2006).

Westin (2006) points out that, unlike other Western European countries, Sweden has a policy of permanent immigration, which treats labour migrants as future citizens. After Sweden joined the EU in 1995 and the setting up of the Schengen scheme in 1996, it seems likely that some SSA migrants have used Sweden as a transit point to other European destinations.

Capacity-building for diaspora organisations in Sweden

The strengths of diaspora NGOs include socio-cultural awareness, specialised knowledge of needs in home communities, ability to work within and between cultures and having the trust of home country communities. But many, especially the smaller, less formal groups, lack capacity in areas like fundraising, strategic planning, monitoring and evaluation and project and financial management (Murray, 2007). The Swedish government should explore avenues to work with these groups: Sweden can build on the skills and talents of migrants to promote the development of their countries of origin, but the first step is for diaspora groups to be better organised and for the extent of their development activity and their potential to be determined (Solidar, 2007). Then, appropriate institutions can assess needs and establish focused means of engagement and impact as the basis of donor-diaspora cooperation.

In 2003, the UK negotiated with diaspora groups and individuals to establish an umbrella body that brings together a diverse array of diaspora, migrant community groups in order to facilitate interaction between diaspora groups and the UK's Department of International Development (Chikezie, 2007). Sweden could perhaps follow this example.

Although not a major player, Sweden could work with other rich countries that are currently depleting SSA of its skilled professionals on ongoing bilateral and multilateral initiatives aimed at attracting back skilled professionals and utilising their expertise. As has been mentioned, residential laws of rich countries should be made more flexible, to give skilled professionals the opportunity of relocating without losing their residence rights in those countries. Moral appeals such as that launched by South Africa to Canada to dissuade the latter country from skimming off its skilled professionals, especially doctors, should be replicated globally. Information about the regulations guiding entry, residence and employment abroad should be disseminated to potential emigrants in countries having, or likely to have, a significant potential emigrant population.

6. Human trafficking

Human trafficking is the dark side of human migration. Deepening poverty, persistent unemployment, conflicts, human deprivation and expectations of a dismal future have fostered an environment in which human trafficking can flourish (ILO 2003). Trafficking in human beings involves mainly women and children, trafficked both within and from Africa, using third party scams involving criminal gangs. Infringing the human rights of its victims, trafficking has assumed alarming global proportions in recent years (Fitzgibbon, 2003).

Three main types of trafficking have been identified, namely trafficking in children, mainly for farm labour and domestic work within and across countries; trafficking in women and young persons for sexual exploitation, mainly outside the region; and trafficking in women from outside the region for the sex industry of South Africa (IOM, 2003; UNICEF, 2003).

Regional details
West Africa
In West Africa, the main source, transit and destination countries for trafficked women and children are Ghana, Nigeria and Senegal. Trafficking in young children from rural areas [?] has increased in recent years, especially from Mali, Benin, Burkina Faso, Togo and Ghana to Côte d'Ivoire's commercial farms, and from and through Nigeria to Gabon. Children are recruited through networks of agents to work as domestic servants, in the informal sector or on plantations. Parents are forced by poverty and ignorance to enlist their children, hoping to benefit from their wages (Human Rights Watch, 2003). UNICEF estimates – though this is highly contestable – that up to 200,000 children are trafficked annually in West and Central Africa (UNICEF, 2003).

Trafficking in girls is reportedly rampant on the Niger/Chad/Nigeria border – the 'triangle of shame'. Hundreds of girls from Edo state, Nigeria, end up in the sex industry in Italy. Women from war-torn Liberia and Sierra Leone work as prostitutes in Mali, just as local Malian women are trafficked to Burkina Faso, Côte d'Ivoire and France. Mali also serves as transit country for women from anglophone countries who are exploited as sex workers in the EU.

East Africa
In East Africa, women and young girls abducted from conflict zones are forced to become sex slaves to rebel commanders or to affluent men in Sudan and the Gulf States. In Kenya, there is trafficking of young girls to Europe by syndicates run by Japanese businessmen, and of girls from India and parts of South Asia into Kenya. Kenya also serves as a transit route for trafficked Ethiopian women to Europe, Lebanon and the Gulf States (Butegwa, 1997). Ethiopia is a source of trafficked women to Lebanon and the Gulf States.

Southern Africa
In Southern Africa, trafficking in women and children for sexual exploitation is a simmering problem, especially in Lesotho, Mozambique, Malawi, South Africa and Zambia, with South Africa a destination for regional and extra-regional trafficking. It is estimated that over 1,000 young women from Bangkok, Hong Kong, Kuala Lumpur and Singapore are trafficked into

South Africa annually through a network of organised syndicates from Thailand, China and Eastern Europe (Selabe, 2000; Martens et al., 2003).

Trafficking outside the region

Faced with strict immigration control measures and tightened barriers to legal entry into Europe, trafficking syndicates have devised complicated itineraries for their victims across many East European countries to their ultimate destination. Women and children are trafficked to Europe (Italy, Germany, Spain, France, Sweden, the UK, Netherlands) for domestic labour, sexual exploitation and pornography. Leaders of trafficking rings or syndicated groups employ intermediaries who make contact with potential migrants, obtain travel documents for them, organise transport and sometimes accompany them to ensure their arrival and compel compliance with the terms of the agreement between smugglers and their victims.

Trafficking syndicates offer jobs in restaurants and hotels to lure unsuspecting young women – for example, from Malawi or Zambia – through Johannesburg to Germany, Belgium or Italy. Before departure, rituals are often performed to frighten the victims into not escaping (IOM, 2003). On arrival in Europe, the young women discover that the promises were bogus and their passports are seized to forestall their escape. Stranded and helpless, they are bonded to work – often as prostitutes – for many years to defray the huge sums demanded by the traffickers (see Adepoju, 2005c for details). If they are apprehended and deported, their reintegration back home is made difficult by the stigma of failure, and local communities are wary of the diseases that they may have contracted abroad. Many victims of trafficking end up engulfed by, rather than escaping from the trap of poverty, resulting in both personal trauma and dishonour to their families.

Root causes of trafficking

Child trafficking in sub-Saharan Africa is a demand-driven phenomenon – the existence of an international market for children in labour and the sex trade coupled with an abundant supply of children from poor families (Veil, 1998). Parents enter contractual arrangements and must provide all or part of the funds for the journey, believing that their children will be assisted with education and jobs abroad. They may also be indebted to the sponsors (Dottridge, 2002).

Child trafficking has also increased as a result of the growing network of intermediaries, the absence of any clear legal framework, the scarcity of trained police to investigate cases of trafficking, the ignorance and complicity of parents, the corruption of border officials and open borders that facilitate transnational movement (Anderson and Davidson, 2003). It should be noted, however, that normal cross-border migration is equallycharacterised by child trafficking

Policy measures

Widespread media coverage of the harrowing experiences of trafficked victims, intensive advocacy by concerned local and international NGOs and case studies of human rights abuses and dangers to trafficked persons in transit and at their destinations have forced many leaders to accept that human trafficking in the region has reached crisis proportions (Adepoju, 2005a).

In Senegal in December 2001, ECOWAS foreign affairs ministers adopted a political declaration and action plan against human trafficking, committing their respective governments to ratifying and fully implementing international instruments to strengthen laws against such trafficking. Training of police, immigration officials, prosecutors and judges and data-gathering are essential components of the plan (Sita, 2003).

West and Central African countries agreed to a platform of action in 2002 to protect child workers, strengthen cooperation between governments and establish transit and reception centres for repatriated children. Benin, Mali, Gabon and Nigeria established interministerial committees to address the issue of child trafficking (Salah, 2004), and Gabon set up a similar national commission. Benin, Togo and Nigeria have strengthened control posts along their common borders to track and repatriate trafficked children.

Many countries find it difficult to control and prevent the smuggling of human beings, partly because they lack the capacity to respond adequately to and also because they have no regulations to deal with it (UNICEF, 2000). In September 2002, an Africa-Europe meeting of experts sponsored by the governments of Sweden and Italy called for a number of measures in countries of origin and destination to combat trafficking and raise awareness, protect and assist victims, create a legislative framework and increase law enforcement. Other countries of destination for African trafficked victims – Spain, the Netherlands and the UK – are implementing similar schemes. But the rich countries need to do more to address the demand side of the phenomenon by, among other measures, collaborating with the source and transit countries to criminalise the trafficking and protect the rights and dignity of victims. Other measures include the repatriation of victims under humane conditions and assistance in their rehabilitation and integration in their home countries.

In general, the demand-reduction strategy for trafficking remains the least developed aspect in many destination countries. Rich destination countries have different policies and laws relating to the commercial sex industry. Variations in conceptual and definitional aspects of forced labour make the adoption of uniform standards of enforcement problematic. In many destination countries, law enforcement against trafficking in persons is ineffective: protection of and support for trafficked victims is inadequate and prosecution of traffickers remains elusive (Wilton Park, 2007). In order to tackle the demand for commercial sex or for cheap labour, public awareness of the plight of trafficked victims is critical and successful prosecution of offenders and protection of victims are essential. International cooperation between countries of origin, transit and destination on trafficking and smuggling of persons must be enforced, with rich countries also providing resources for equipment and capacity-building of law enforcement officials in originating countries.

Data on trafficking and legal framework

Data on trafficking remain extremely poor, so details on trafficking within or outside the region are incomplete. The dozen or so studies conducted in SSA countries are small-scale, covering areas seen as recruiting grounds for trafficking (Adepoju, 2005a). There is an urgent need to improve data-gathering. Cooperative research and information-sharing between countries of origin, transit and destination on the numbers and nationalities of trafficked persons and on smuggling routes should be encouraged, as well as tracer studies of trafficked victims.

Together with weak enforcement of existing laws, the absence of judicial frameworks limits attempts to arrest, prosecute and punish traffickers in human beings (Pearson, 2002).

It is imperative that governments strengthen or enact relevant laws and legal frameworks and empower their law enforcement agencies to deal swiftly and successfully with such matters.

More important is the protection and rehabilitation of victims. In South Africa, for instance, trafficked women, mostly prostitutes apprehended by security forces, are simply deported to their home countries as irregular immigrants – because of a lack of domestic legal instruments for criminalising trafficking – as is indeed the case in other parts of SSA as well.

Public awareness

Research indicates that about half of sub-Saharan-African countries recognise trafficking as a problem and that child trafficking is perceived as more severe than trafficking in women. In West and Central Africa more than 70 per cent of countries identified trafficking as a problem, compared to only one-third in East and Southern Africa (UNICEF, 2003).

Political leaders across the region are becoming more conscious of the acuteness of the problem of human trafficking and countries are starting to adopt action plans at national, bilateral and multilateral levels. The general public, on the other hand, is not sufficiently aware of the extent to which organised criminal groups are involved, or of the fate of the victims of trafficking. Even the parents or guardians of trafficked children do not realise the severe exploitation to which their wards are often subjected.

7. Legislative framework governing migration in sub-Saharan Africa

Regional initiatives

Sub-regional economic organisations or unions – such as ECOWAS and the Southern African Development Community (SADC) – are potential avenues for multinational cooperation and policy development on migration, especially in cases where migrations to a single country preponderate. The prosperity of many of these countries was built on migrant labour: in cocoa and coffee plantations in Ghana and Côte d'Ivoire, mines and agriculture in South Africa and forestry and oil in Gabon. Resource-rich but labour-short countries such as Botswana, Gabon and Côte d'Ivoire rely heavily on immigrant labour. Other 'magnet-countries' are Kenya and Nigeria (Adepoju, 2000).

The growing number of migrants and the complexity of migratory configurations have resulted in several initiatives and regional consultative processes under the auspices of the Berne Initiative. These provide a forum for the exchange of information, experiences and perspectives, and facilitate cooperation, capacity building and dialogue between governments (Adepoju, 2004a). Now is the time for these regional groupings to shift the focus from controlling to managing migration, so that standards agreed upon globally have a greater chance of successful implementation. Regional details are now discussed.

ECOWAS free movement of persons

The ECOWAS protocol of May 1979 on free movement of persons and the right of residence and establishment formalised the free movement of ECOWAS citizens within member countries and has been acclaimed as a trend-setter in migration policy development and management (Adepoju, 2007a). Community citizens in possession of valid travel documentation can enter member states without a visa for up to 90 days (ECOWAS, 1999; 2004), though member states may refuse admission to would-be immigrants deemed 'inadmissible' under their laws. The second phase (right of residence), which came into force in July 1986, and the revised treaty of 1992 affirmed the right of Community citizens to enter and reside in other member states. ECOWAS passports are to progressively replace national passports over a transitional period of ten years.

Modernisation of border procedures through the training of immigration officials and the use of passport scanning machines should reduce delays and eliminate extortion (Adepoju, 2002). ECOWAS travellers cheques and a common currency, too, have been designed to facilitate cross-border movement (Adepoju, 2004b). National laws and employment and investment codes that restrict 'foreigners' from participating in certain economic activities are being harmonised through regional and sub-regional treaties to ensure the rights of migrant workers within host countries (UN, 2004).

SADC and COMESA

A protocol on the free movement of persons within the Common Market of Eastern and Southern Africa (COMESA) and SADC's lacklustre attempts to facilitate intra-Community movement of nationals are largely still on the drawing board. Migration is a controversial issue in SADC countries: the 1997 protocol on the free movement of persons was revised several times to incorporate objections, especially from South Africa (Solomon, 1997). In the revised, 'Facilitation of Movement of Persons' protocol, the six-month visa-free period has been reduced to 90 days per year, and states have reserved the right to determine conditions of entry of immigrants (Oucho and Crush, 2001). The protocol, which remained stalled at the political level for a long time, was eventually signed by member states in mid-August 2005.

East African Community

An East African Community (EAC) protocol on the free movement of persons, labour and services, and the right of establishment and residence is being developed under the International Labour Organization (ILO) Labour Migration Project for Integration and Development, supported by the EU. Employers and trade unions are playing an active role in the process of formalising the protocol on the free circulation of persons, labour and services and rights of establishment and residence within the Community (ILO, 2004). On 1 July 2007, Burundi and Rwanda formally joined the EAC.

Capacity building

Capacity building of immigration officials is a critical and urgent issue. They presently function as border control and security, but their role needs to be transformed into one of migration management – helping to facilitate rather than restrict regular migration and regional integration. Migration management is a complex process that goes beyond punitive measures and instruments of control, and retraining must focus on national laws and treaties and regional protocols and take into account the diverse elements of migration management.

Collaboration and cooperation

The 2005 GCIM report correctly concluded that migration cannot be managed effectively through unilateral action. Countries can simultaneously be the point of origin, transit and destination, so bilateral relations should be forged among the various countries in regions and sub-regions, as well as multilaterally through ECOWAS, SADC, EAC, the EU, the African, Caribbean and Pacific (ACP) group of countries, and so on.

At the national level, collaboration between government agencies dealing with migration matters is essential but rarely exists at the moment. The key role of trade relations, and especially the effects – both short- and long-term – of trade agreements on migration is not yet appreciated by many migration stakeholders and should be explicitly recognised.

There is a need for ongoing dialogue between the various stakeholders to discuss approaches to migration concerns, share ideas and enhance cooperation in migration management. Such processes could lead to the development of coherent policy frameworks for the management of migration.

8. Principal actors in migration issues in sub-Saharan Africa

The role of development partners

Rich countries engage in the direct recruitment of professionals through what is seen by many as unfair competition, deciding how many workers to recruit and where. As already noted, highly qualified professionals with internationally marketable skills are a small proportion of the emigrants from any given country, but their loss costs poor countries in a variety of ways, not least the opportunity to train replacement cohorts.

As the 2005 GCIM report noted, national governance of international migration faces four major challenges. The report listed, *inter alia*, the following needs:
- for migration to form an integral part of every country's national economic and development plan, to address the need for coherence in migration policies rather than competing priorities;
- for harmonising coordination between ministries responsible for migration matters, and for adequate consultation between government, the corporate sector and civil society;
- for enhancing the capacity and knowledge of institutions dealing with migration issues, to maximise the benefits derivable from human mobility; and
- for inter-state cooperation and shared responsibility.

The recommendation is for governments to provide prospective migrants, especially temporary contract workers, with orientation and training courses before their departure, so that they have a better understanding of their rights and obligations and are better equipped to cope with working in a foreign country (GCIM, 2005). This is most apt, especially for sending countries whose nationals often have exaggerated expectations about conditions in rich countries.

It is significant that the receiving countries of the EU have been the prime architects of migration management schemes, initiating the bilateral agreements, their content, the modalities for their implementation, and providing funds to persuade sending countries to fall in line and implement the agreements. Sending countries do not seem to have sufficiently critical input into the negotiations leading to agreements: little wonder then that some of the earlier agreements have not been implemented.

Other internal and external actors

Although states retain the power to decide who enters the country and under what conditions, a wide range of civil society organisations (CSOs), international organisations and financial institutions and the private sector are increasingly engaged in migration matters. The choices that the powerful private sector actors make have huge implications – for instance in outsourcing white-collar jobs, which produces different patterns of migration for skilled and semi-skilled persons. People to whom work does not come may choose to move to new outsourcing centres.

The Business Sector

Business, particularly the professional sector, benefits from multinational skilled labour and is part of the cause of the brain drain. It must, therefore, play its part in developing pragmatic approaches and solutions to highly skilled migration from poor countries. The 'world-wide workers' labour database, an internet job site for the oil and gas industry, which facilitates the matching of employers and potential employees worldwide, could be placed in this context. As part of its corporate social responsibility (CSR) function, business must build partnerships with CSOs and governments to match the demand and supply of skills, minimise brain waste, promote the human rights of skilled migrants, help create an economic climate conducive to domestic employment generation and assist in the return of skills (Adepoju, 2007a).

The business sector can also partner with governments to improve working conditions in countries of origin and enhance productivity through higher remuneration, restoring dilapidated equipment and infrastructure and promoting workers' rights – to retain highly-skilled workers. The challenges are to achieve effective collaboration among non-state actors themselves and between non-state actors and governmental institutions.

Civil Society Organisations

Among the actions they could take in sending and receiving countries, CSOs should organise pre-departure advocacy workshops on conditions in the destination country and checks for relevant migration documents. In addition, NGOs can partner with governments to monitor the work of recruitment agencies by establishing procedures and standards, for example ensuring that recruitment agencies check that the correct work conditions are in place before migrants leave home, and setting up cultural orientation programmes. These are some of the recommendations of the Civil Society Day to the recently-held Global Forum on Migration and Development in Brussels.

International Financial Institutions

External factors are also to blame for the negative impact of government policies that prompt the exodus of skilled professionals. Fiscal policies imposed by international financial institutions (IMF, World Bank) restrict provision for health and education in poor countries and often encourage the brain drain. In many SSA countries, for instance, despite a shortage of nurses in public facilities, many nurses are either unemployed or work outside the health sector – because of a freeze on recruitment.

International agencies

The ILO's tripartite model for consultation can be adopted in dealing with issues such as the residency status of skilled migrants, work permits, developing codes of practice against racism in the workplace, promoting CSR and monitoring compliance of the private sector (both employers and recruiters) with approved codes of practice. Agreements could extend union membership, improve protection of migrant workers and use collective bargaining to ensure equal rights for foreign professionals and their treatment on a par with nationals.

Lessons learnt

Bilateral and multilateral agreements between countries that send and receive migrants must address the issue of depleting SSA of its scarce skilled-manpower resources. It is important that residency laws of rich countries be made flexible, to give skilled professionals an opportunity to relocate without losing their residence rights in those countries.

Sub-Saharan African countries need to ensure that their interests and concerns are adequately reflected in any migration negotiations. Issues relating to the treatment of their nationals living and working in regular situations in EU countries, the rights of irregular migrants to basic services and the need to review unfair trade regimes that impoverish millions engaged in farming at home should assume centre stage in future migration discussions. Efforts should be made to revisit existing agreements, to review and amend unfavourable conditions. Above all, the embassies and missions of SSA countries in destination countries should provide their nationals with information on the rules that guide entry, residence and work – in short, their rights and obligations in receiving societies.

9. Migration and development: challenges and prospects

Trade and migration
The debate on trade regimes is of particular importance to poor countries. The World Bank estimates that high tariffs and technical barriers to trade cost SSA countries about US$20 billion yearly in lost exports. A viable strategy for enhancing economic growth and generating employment is the opening up of markets of the North to exports from developing countries and the removal of import tariffs (UN, 2006a). These objectives have informed the ACP group's renegotiation of trade and aid agreements with the EU under the Lome Convention (Lome 5).

The agricultural protectionist policies of the richest countries, especially the US and Europe, have a negative effect on the income of farmers in the sub-region. For example, farm subsidies on cotton in the US have artificially spurred local production levels and depressed world prices: in 2001 the US spent more subsidising 25,000 cotton farmers than it did on its entire aid budget for Africa (Stiglitz, 2006b). This meant a loss of US$301 million by African exporters – with Burkina Faso, Mali and Benin each losing about 2 per cent of GDP growth – and the impoverishment of more than 10 million sub-Saharan African farmers who will now migrate into urban unemployment, making some of them potential emigrants. The clamour by African, Asian and Latin American leaders to achieve mutually beneficial trade relations should be placed in this context: deepening poverty has frustrated recent achievements in democratic and economic reform as well as hampered efforts to improve living conditions, stimulate economic growth and generate employment.

Preferential trade can affect emigration pressure from poor countries. The lesson to be learnt from the collapse of the WTO Doha negotiations in 2006 is that political will must be mustered to open the markets of rich countries to exports from developing countries and to remove tariffs on imports of labour-intensive goods produced in poor countries. Donors should use ODAs to improve infrastructure for human capital development and support growth policies, thus increasing domestic development and decreasing pressure to emigrate.

Globalisation with a human face
Increasing restrictions on regular migration are partly to blame for the rise in irregular migration. Rich countries need migrants to meet labour shortages in highly skilled areas and to fill unskilled jobs that locals do not want (Legrain, 2007). Faced with rising domestic unemployment among 'underutilised' workers, rich countries have become increasingly selective, opting mainly for migrants with skills. In poor SSA countries, where emigration helps to reduce domestic unemployment and boosts revenue through migrants' remittances, governments are intensely worried about the detrimental effect of the loss of skilled workers on the achievement of MDG. While it poses real policy challenges, migration has immense potential for migrants and for countries of origin and destination. The real challenge is how to develop an international framework to manage migration in a comprehensive manner and promote globalisation with a human face (Stiglitz, 2006a).

Reducing emigration pressure and providing employment for youths
A major development issue is the productive employment of the millions of educated youths scrambling for work in SSA, and for that reason the region is likely to become one of the

largest sources of potential emigration. The capacity of SSA governments to generate viable employment for its youth is further weakened by the limited size of internal markets, especially in the new era of globalisation. Irregular migrants pay US$1,500 to US$4,000 to smugglers in attempts to enter Europe clandestinely. Such huge sums of money could be used productively as start-up for small enterprises (Adepoju, 2006b). In that regard, the energy deficit has to be dealt with to ensure that small enterprises can thrive. Governments should tap into the resilience and determination of youths and support them in self-employment rather than allow them to perish in the desert or the sea in a desperate search for the illusory Golden Fleece.

Sub-Saharan African migration is mainly South-South, but since the late 19080s traditional labour-importing countries have experienced endemic political and economic crises, spurring out-migration of their nationals. That pressure can be eased by putting in place mechanisms allowing for more regular immigration, thus improving the lives of immigrants and, through remittances, of those left behind. This resonates with intervention programmes designed to reduce emigration pressures at regional source.

The North should factor into its development programme cooperation and dialogue with or through the vibrant SSA diaspora associations active in development projects at home, to provide matching grants or micro loans to local projects – such as the irrigation schemes in Mali and Senegal that were sponsored by emigrants. They should also work with financial institutions to reduce the costs and risks to migrants in remitting transfers. More important still is the need to remove the high tariffs and technical barriers to trade that cost the sub-region billions of dollars in lost exports. This would provide much-needed revenue for development and employment-generation, thus reducing emigration pressure.

Sub-Saharan African governments for their part should institute incentive-based tax regimes to attract migrants' remittances and ensure their productive, employment-generating investment. Assistance in job creation projects must become the cornerstone of the region's development agenda. Mutually beneficial trade relations with rich countries is key to improved living conditions, economic growth and employment opportunities. For this to be possible, both South and North must make concerted efforts to resolve the region's contagious conflicts: the absence of peace and stability discourages investment and leads to capital flight – and the resulting lack of economic alternatives prompts emigration.

Research and data on migration

Data on migration within and outside sub-Saharan Africa are patchy, but slowly improving. At the moment, information on the stock and flow of emigrants from the region is more readily available in the destination countries than in the countries of origin. SSA countries need to institutionalise the collection of data on internal, intra-regional and international migration, and to endeavour to keep track of the number and characteristics of their nationals emigrating abroad. A modest start has begun in SADC with the round of censuses for 2000 that collected information on cross-border migrations, but such data must be analysed and widely disseminated.

The collection of up-to-date information on migration will have to be factored into data-gathering procedures. Censuses are the most comprehensive data source but they need to be supplemented by the collection, dissemination and use of special collaborative border survey data. To ensure coherent migration policies, current data-collection methods must be reviewed, updated and expanded, and agencies responsible for migration matters must coordinate their activities more effectively.

To provide planners, politicians and policy makers with comprehensive data on migration dynamics, cross-country collaborative research – using innovative approaches to capture emerging and changing configurations – is required on a number of themes. Foremost among these is the interlinked factors that drive traditional and changing migratory flows in various contexts in the region. Of special policy concern is the independent migration of female professionals and its impact on gender roles, as well as on family, social and development policies (Adepoju, 2006f). Since migration in SSA is essentially intraregional, policy research must also address the causes of the region's contagious conflicts. As already noted, peace and stability are prerequisites for investment, development and employment generation, and good governance can help curtail skills flight and the exiling of the intelligentsia.

The short-to-long term effects of the emigration of skilled professionals on healthcare delivery, including training and manpower development, especially in an era of HIV/AIDS pandemic, is a major challenge for researchers. As already mentioned, they must explore strategies to minimise the outflow, retain, attract back and effectively utilise the skills of these professionals. This also requires a skills audit of the diaspora to ascertain their number, location, current skills profiles, qualifications on arrival, job placements, training and experience gained. In addition, such an audit must monitor the role of these professionals in the development of their home countries through home improvement associations, skills and technology transfer, transnational trade links, advocacy and other linkages. Evidence-based research is required on lessons learnt from the IOM's Return and Re-integration of Qualified Nationals programme and other schemes for facilitating the return, retention and reintegration of nationals and promoting their potential for country-of-origin development.

Collaborative, longitudinal tracer studies are required and/or should be expanded to capture adequately the dynamics of remittances (especially by second generation and independent female migrants), their intended and actual use and their impact at individual, family and community levels.

Cooperation between governments is crucial in combating trafficking. Cooperative research and information-sharing between countries of origin and destination should be strongly encouraged. There should in addition be increased operational contact between law enforcement authorities of recipient countries in order to share information on numbers and nationalities of trafficked persons, smuggling routes and methods of interdiction. Cooperation between researchers in countries of origin and destination, with a focus on tracer studies of trafficked victims, is desirable. Above all, linkages between countries of destination and origin must be established and reinforced.

The medium-to-long-term social, economic and demographic implications of the HIV/AIDS pandemic on the supply of skilled workers in heavily infected countries must be explored more systematically. This applies also to the tendency to resort to immigration to offset domestic labour supply losses. Current research efforts have focused largely on the demographic consequences of HIV/AIDS: attention should now shift to the economic and social consequences on the productive sectors at micro (household), meso (community) and macro (national) levels (Adepoju, 2006d).

In Southern Africa, high HIV/AIDS prevalence is creating a nightmare scenario of acute labour shortages. The pandemic in this region is taking a heavy toll on the education sector of traditional sending countries. The emigration of skilled health professionals, too, is occurring at a time when their services are acutely required in the overstressed health sector. The role of migration in spreading HIV/AIDS should also be re-examined critically: immigrants are uniformly blamed, but the evidence for their being the prime vector of the disease is untested and such claims may well be spurious.

The future outlook

Migration and development policies would have a better chance of succeeding if the dynamics and underlying factors of migration, in both countries of origin and of destination, were fully taken into account (Van Dalen and Esveldt, 2003). Sub-Saharan Africa is facing daunting challenges in respect of increasing irregular migration, migrants' rights, human trafficking and the emigration of skilled professionals. Migration issues can no longer be handled only bilaterally: what is needed is a comprehensive approach through global harmonisation of migration policies (Farrant et al., 2006). Global networks are used for trafficking and irregular migration and a global approach is needed to curtail them, with the support of international organisations and governments and taking advantage of the current increase in dialogue among countries.

The seemingly intractable problems posed by migration, circulation, permanent residence and settlement are quite different for each migratory configuration within the different sub-regions, and even within individual countries, and policy responses to them must also differ. The situation, nevertheless, calls for the development of the coordinated implementation of policies and programmes and a comprehensive framework to address issues of migration (AUC, 2004).

In SSA, the number of US$2-a-day workers reached a record high of 26 million in 2006. As the recent ILO report (2007) emphasised, tackling the 'decent work deficit' is a regional and global priority.

A forum for migration dialogue

There is no formal forum within the SSA region specifically for the discussion of migration matters by all stakeholders – including, in particular, the media and the public – as a continuous process, to help dispel the misrepresentations, ignorance and xenophobia that currently surround these issues. Discourses on migration, especially at the receiving end, are full of anxiety, misconception, myth and prejudice, and are fed on xenophobia (see Heran, 2004). The positive aspects of migrants as agents of development in source and destination countries should be made explicit. Consultations between the various stakeholders could lead to the development of a coherent policy framework for the management of migration.

Dialogue and cooperation between the EU and SSA countries is generally weak or non-existent. Policy dialogue can engage all stakeholders in matters of migration management, and this must be institutionalised. Those who should be involved – often with conflicting interests – include the government sector (ministries of labour, trade, home affairs, integration, foreign affairs, justice and so on), the private sector, civil society, trade unions, employers' organisations and the media.

Circularity

To the extent that it confers benefits on the point of destination, circular migration can be promoted. Migrant-receiving countries in Europe need to explore avenues for temporary regular migration as a means of reducing irregular migration by desperate youths, with all the associated consequences and costs of policing irregular migration. There are encouraging signs that, if well managed, migration can result in advantages for all.

Public enlightenment

Sub-Saharan African governments must address ongoing misinformation regarding migration through intensive advocacy programmes to demystify the perception of youths that the roads of EU countries are paved with gold. Appropriate information must be provided, in collaboration with EU embassies and SSA missions abroad, on conditions governing entry, residence and work in various destination countries. Youths generally rely on information from their peers, but such information tends to be distorted, exaggerated and misleading and peer influence remains strong.

Institutional capacity-building

In many countries, the institutional capacity required to manage migratory flows and for effective policy implementation is weak and must be strengthened through the training and/or retraining of officials. At the national level, collaboration between and within agencies of government dealing with migration is essential, but rarely exists at the moment. The key role of trade relations, especially the short- and long-term effects of trade agreements, is not yet evident or appreciated by many migration stakeholders and needs to be explicitly recognised.

10. Conclusion

Migration has hitherto been viewed as problematic, and policies were accordingly formulated to restrict the entry of so-called unwanted migrants to the North. In sub-Saharan Africa, migration has been primarily intra-regional, but globalisation and internal and external factors have prompted the migration of skilled and unskilled migrants, male and female, to the North, in regular and irregular circumstances.

The key message that migration is inherent and inevitable in an inter-connected world is at last starting to get through to all concerned, and so are the potential benefits of migration to migrants and to countries of origin and destination. It is also being recognised that success in managing migration must be anchored in collaboration between sending, transit and receiving countries, as well as in reducing the push factors that prompt it in the first place. Coping with the upsurge in migration must also include creating avenues for regular migration for both skilled and unskilled migrants, for instance by exploring opportunities for circular migration.

These challenges are aggravated by the ageing of populations in the North and the spiralling growth of populations and hence of the labour force in SSA. The journey so far has been tortuous but the deliberations and conclusions of the most recent series of regional and international dialogues on migration and development represent a glimmer of light at the end of the tunnel.

References

Adegbola, O. 1990. *Demographic Effects of Economic Crisis in Nigeria: The Brain Drain Component.* Conference on the Role of Migration in African Development: Issues and Policies for the '90s, Spontaneous Paper. Dakar: Union for African Population Studies.

Adekanye, J. Bayo, 1998. Conflicts, Loss of State Capacities and Migration in Contemporary Africa. In Appleyard, R. (ed.), *Emigration Dynamics in Developing Countries: Vol. 1: Sub-Saharan Africa.* Aldershot: Ashgate.

Adepoju, A. 1988a. International Migration in Africa South of the Sahara. In Appleyard, R. (ed.), *International Migration Today: Trends and Prospects, Vol. 1.* Paris: UNESCO.

—, 1988b. Labour Migration and Employment of ECOWAS Nationals in Nigeria. In Fashoyin, T. (ed.), *Labour and Development in Nigeria.* Lagos: Landmark Publications.

—, 1998. *Links between Internal and International Migration: The African Situation* (first published 1984). Selected articles to commemorate 50th Anniversary of International Social Science Journal. Paris: UNESCO.

—, 2000. Regional Integration, Continuity and Changing Patterns of Intra-regional Migration in Sub-Saharan Africa. In Siddique, M.A.B. (ed.), *International Migration into the 21st century: Essays in honour of Reginald Appleyard.* Aldershot: Edward Edgar

—, 2001. *Population and Sustainable Development in Africa in the 21st century: Challenges and Prospects.* HRDC African Policy Research Series No. 1. Lagos: Concept Publications.

—, 2002. Fostering Free Movements of Persons in West Africa: Achievements, Constraints and Prospects for International Migration. *International Migration*, 40 2:3–28.

—, 2003. Continuity and Changing Configurations of Migration To and From the Republic of South Africa. *International Migration*, 41(1).

—, 2004a. *Regional Migration Processes, Multilateral and Bilateral Migration Agreements in Sub-Saharan Africa.* International Organisation for Migration: Initiative Policy Research Papers. Berne: IOM.

—, 2004b. Trends in International Migration in and from Africa. In Massey, D.S. and Taylor, J.E. (eds), *International Migration Prospects and Policies in a Global Market.* Oxford: Oxford University Press.

—, 2005a. Patterns of Migration in West Africa. In Manuh, T. (ed.), *At Home in the World? International Migration and Development in Contemporary Ghana and West Africa.* Accra: Sub-Saharan Publishers.

—, 2005b. Perspectives on Migration Within and From sub-Saharan Africa. Background paper for the *Conference on Policy Coherence for Development: the African Experience*, 3–4 November. Paris: Organisation for Economic Cooperation and Development.

—, 2005c. Review of Research Data on Trafficking in Sub-Saharan Africa. *International Migration,* 43(1 and 2).

—, 2006a. *African Families in the Twenty-first Century: Prospects and Challenges.* New York: iUniverse.

—, 2006b. The Challenge of Labour Migration Flows between West Africa and the Maghreb. Migration Research Papers. Geneva: International Labour Organisation.

—, 2006c. Internal and International Migration within Africa. In Kok, P.D., Gelderblom, J., Oucho, J. and van Zyl, J. (eds), *Migration in South and Southern Africa: Dynamics and Determinants.* Cape Town: Human Sciences Research Council.

—, 2006d. Leading Issues in International Migration in sub-Saharan Africa. In Cross. C., Gelderblom, J., Roux, N. and Mafukdize, J. (eds), *Views on Migration in Sub-Saharan Africa: Proceedings of an African Migration Alliance Workshop.* Pretoria: Human Sciences Research Council.

—, 2006e. Recent Trends in International Migration In and From Africa. Background Papers No. 1: CeSPI and SID: International Conference on Migration and Development: Opportunities and Challenges for Euro-African Relations: Rome, 6–8 July.

—, 2006f. Policy-driven Research on International Migration in sub-Saharan Africa. In Tamas, K. and Joakim P. (eds), *How Migration can Benefit Development: Bridging the Research and Policy Gap.* Stockholm: Institute for Futures Studies.

—, 2007. *Highly Skilled Migration: Balancing Interests and Responsibilities and Tackling Brain Drain.* Global Forum on Migration and Development: Brussels: Civil Society Day.

—, 2007a. Creating a Borderless West Africa: Constraints and Prospects for Intra-regional Migration. In Pecoud, A. and de Gucheneire, P. (eds), *Migration Without Borders: Essays on the Free Movement of People.* New York/Oxford: Berghahn (with UNESCO).

—, 2007b. Perspectives on International Migration and National Development in sub-Saharan Africa. In Adepoju, A., van Naerssen, T. and Zoomers, A. (eds), *International Migration and National Development in sub-Saharan Africa.* Leiden: Afrika-Studiecentrum Series.

—, and Hammar T. (eds), 1996. *International Migration In and From Africa: Dimension, Challenges and Prospects.* Dakar: PHRDA/Stockholm: CEIFO.

African Diaspora Summit 2003. *African Diaspora Summit, the Netherlands,* Conference proceedings. Amsterdam, 16 December 2003. www.afroneth/messagel.html.

Anarfi, J. and Kwankye, S. with Ofuso-Mensah, A. and Tiemoko, R. 2003. *Migration From and To Ghana: A Background Paper,* Working Paper C4. University of Sussex, Development Research Centre on Migration, Globalisation and Poverty.

Anderson, B. and Davidson, J.O. 2003. *Is Trafficking in Human Beings Demand Driven? A Multi-country Pilot Study.* IOM Migration Research Series No. 15. Geneva: IOM.

AU (African Union) 2006. Draft African Common Position on Migration and Development. *Report of Experts' Meeting on Migration and Development*, Algiers, 3–5 April.

AUC (African Union Commission) 2004. Draft Strategic Framework for a Policy on Migration in Africa. Report of Experts' Group Meeting on Policy Framework on Migration in Africa, Addis Ababa, 29–30 March. Addis Ababa: AUC Social Affairs Department.

Azam, J.P. and Gubert, F. 2005. *Migrant Remittances and Economic Development in Africa: A Review of Evidence*. Paper prepared for the African Economic Research Consortium Plenary Session, Nairobi, 29 May. http://idei.fr/doc/wp/2005/remit.pdf (accessed July 2007).

Bach, S. 2003. *International Migration of Health Workers: Labour and Social Issues.* Sectoral Activities Programme, Working Paper 209, Geneva: ILO.

Black, R., King, R. and Litchfield J., with Ammassari, S. and Tiemoko, R. 2004. *Transnational Migration, Return and Development in West Africa*. University of Sussex, Centre for Migration Research and Poverty.

Block, A. 2005. *The Development Potential of Zimbabweans in the Diaspora: A Survey of Zimbabweans living in the UK and South Africa*. Geneva: IOM.

Boubakri, H. 2004. *Transit Migration between Tunisia, Libya and Sub-Saharan Africa: Study Based on Greater Tunis*. Paper for Regional Conference on Migrants in Transit Countries: Sharing Responsibility for Management and Protection. Istanbul 30 September–1 October. http://www.coe.int/t/f/coh%E9sion_sociale/migrations/MG-RCONF_2004_ 6e (accessed July 2007).

Buchan, J. 2002. *International Recruitment of Nurses: A United Kingdom Case Study*. Edinburgh: Queen Margaret University College.

—, and Dovlo, D. 2004. *International Recruitment of Health Workers in the UK*. London: Department for International Development, Health Systems Resource Centre.

Bump, M. 2006. Ghana: Searching for Opportunities at Home and Abroad. *Migration Information Source*, March. http://www.migrationinformation.org/Profiles/display.cfm? ID=381 (accessed July 2007).

Butegwa, F. 1997. Trafficking in Women in Africa: A Regional Report (mimeographed).

Campbell, E.K. 2003. Attitudes of Botswana Citizens towards Immigrants: Signs of Xenophobia? *International Migration*, 41(4):71–109.

Carling, J. 2002. Cape Verde: Towards the End of Emigration? *Migration Information Source*, November.

—, 2006 *Migration, Human Smuggling and Trafficking from Nigeria to Europe*. Research Series No. 23. Geneva: IOM.

Chikezie, C.E. 2007. *Strategies for Building Diaspora/Migrant Organisation Capacity for Development*. Global Forum on Migration and Development: Brussels: Civil Society Day.

Chilivumbo, A. 1985. Malawi's Labour Migration to the South: An Historical

Review. In *Migratory Labour in Southern Africa*. Addis Ababa: UNECA.

Chishti, M. 2007. The Rise in Remittances to India: A Closer Look. *Migration Information Source*, February.

Clearfield, E. and Batalova, J. 2007. Foreign-Born Health-Care Workers in the United States. *Migration Information Source*, July. http://www.migrationinformation.org/development.cfm (accessed July 2007).

Commission of the European Communities, 2007. *Communication from the Commission to the European Parliament and the Council: From Cairo to Lisbon – The EU-African Strategic Partnership*. Brussels

Commonwealth Secretariat 2003. Commonwealth Code of Practice for the International Recruitment of Health Workers. London: Commonwealth Secretariat. http://www.plexusrecruitment.com.au/resource/Commonwealth_Code_of_Practice.pdf (accessed July 2007).

Crisp, J. 2006. *Forced Displacement in Africa: Dimensions, Difficulties and Policy Directions*. Background Paper No. 4: CeSPI and SID International Conference on Migration and Development, Rome, 6–8 July. http://www.sidint.org/migration/BG4_Crisp.pdf (accessed July 2007).

D'Onofrio, L. (ed.) 2001. *Migration, Return and Development in West Africa*. Report of Workshop, 25 May 2001. University of Sussex, Transrede Research Project.

De Fletter, F. 1986. Recent Trends and Prospects of Black Migration to South Africa. *Journal of Modern African Studies*, 23(4).

Dottridge, M. 2002. Trafficking in Children in West and Central Africa. *Gender and Development*, 10(1):38–49.

ECA 1981. *International Migration Trends and their Implications*, African Population Studies Series No. 4. Population Division, ECA. Addis Ababa: Economic Commission for Africa.

ECOWAS (Economic Community of West African States) 1999. *An ECOWAS Compendium on Free Movement, Right of Residence and Establishment*. Abuja, Nigeria: ECOWAS.

—, 2004. *West African Integration Perspectives – Searching for a New Development Model*. Annual Report of the Executive Secretary, ECOWAS. Abuja, Nigeria: ECOWAS.

European Commission, 2005. *Visit to Ceuta and Melilla – Mission Report Technical Mission to Morocco on Illegal Immigration (7–11 October 2005) MEMO/05/380*. Brussels.

Farrant, M., MacDonald, A. and Sriskandarajah, D. 2006. *Migration and Development: Opportunities and Challenges for Policymakers*, IOM Migration Research Series No. 22. Geneva: International Organization for Migration.

Findley, S.E. 1997. Migration and Family Interactions in Africa. In Adepoju, A. (ed.), *Family, Population and Development in Africa*. London/New Jersey: Zed.

—, Traore, S., Ouedraogo, D. and Diarra, S. 1995. Emigration from the Sahel. *International Migration*, 33(3 and 4):469–520.

Fitzgibbon, K. 2003. Modern-Day Slavery? The Scope of Trafficking in Persons in Africa. *African Security Review*, 12(1).

Follow-up Meeting of the Euro-African Conference 'Migration and Development' www.maec.gov.ma/migration/doc

GCIM (Global Commission on International Migration) 2005. *Migration in an Inter-connected World: New Directions for Action*. Geneva: GCIM.

Ghanaian Government 2001. *Homecoming Summit*. www.homecoming.com.gh/summitpackage.html.

Ghosh, B. 2006. *Migrants' Remittances and Development: Myths, Rhetoric and Realities*. Geneva: International Organization for Migration (with The Hague Process on Refugees and Migration).

Heran, F. 2004. Five Immigration Myths. *Bulletin Mensuel d'Information de l'Institut National d'Études Démographique: Population and Societies*, No. 397 (January).

Horowitz, S. and Kaplan, D.E. 2001. The Jewish Exodus from the New South Africa: Realities and Implications. *International Migration* 39(3):3–32.

Human Rights Watch 2003. Borderline Slavery: Child Trafficking in Togo. Human Rights Watch 15 (8A). http://hrw.org/reports/2003/togo0403/ (accessed July 2007).

IEMed (European Institute of the Mediterranean) 2004. *Rethinking Migration Policies*. World Congress, Human Movements and Immigration. Barcelona 2–5 September.

ILO (International Labour Organisation) 2003. *Trafficking in Human Beings: New Approaches to Combating the Problem*. ILO: Geneva. http://www.ilo.org/dyn/declaris/DECLARATIONWEB.DOWNLOAD_BLOB?Var_DocumentID=1871 (accessed July 2007).

—, 2004a. *Declaration on Employment and Poverty Alleviation in Africa*. Issues Paper, Extraordinary Summit of African Union Heads of State and Governments, Ouagadougou, September. ILO.

—, 2004b. *ILO-EU/EAC Labour Migration Project, East Africa. Summary, Conclusions, Recommendations and the Way Forward*. ILO Launch and Stakeholders' Meeting, Arusha, 13–16 December. Nairobi: ILO.

—, 2004c. *A Fair Globalization: Creating Opportunities for All*. Report by the World Commission on the Social Dimension on Globalization. Geneva: ILO.

—, 2006. Report: Africa-Europe Inter-regional Dialogue: Labour Migration for Integration and Development. Brussels: ILO.

—, 2007. *Global Employment Trends Brief 2007*. ILO: Geneva.

IOM (International Organisation for Migration) 2001. Trafficking of Women from Ethiopia: Report of National Workshop. Addis Ababa, 22–23 February.

—, 2003. The Trafficking of Women and Children in the Southern African Region, Presentation of Research Findings, Geneva: IOM. http://www.old.iom.int/documents/publication/en/southernafrica_trafficking.pdf (accessed July 2007)

—, 2004. *Migration for Development in Africa*, General Strategy Paper. Geneva: IOM.

King Baudouin Foundation, 2007. Report of the Civil Society Day of the Global Forum on Migration and Development, Brussels

Koser, K. (ed.) 2003. *New African Diasporas*. London: Routledge.

Le Courier, 1997. *Reportage: Gabon*. African Caribbean Pacific, No. 165, Sept–Oct 1997.

Lefko-Everett, K. 2004. Botswana's Changing Migration Patterns. *Migration Information Source*, September.

Legrain, P. 2007. *Immigrants: Your Country Needs Them*. London: Little, Brown.

Makinwa-Adebusoye, P. K. 1990. Female Migration in Africa: An Overview. In *The Role of Migration in African Development: Issues and Policies for the 90s. UAPS Commissioned Papers*. Dakar: Union for African Population Studies.

Martens, J., Pieczkowiski, M.M. and van Vuuren-Smyth, B. 2003. *Seduction, Sale and Slavery: Trafficking in Women and Children for Sexual Exploitation in Southern Africa*, Pretoria: IOM Regional Office for Southern Africa.

Martin, P., Martin, S. and Cross, S. 2007. High-level Dialogue on Migration and Development. *International Migration*, 45(1):7–25.

Mayer, J.-B. 2001. Network Approach versus Brain Drain: Lessons from the Diaspora. *International Migration*, 39(5):91–110.

Mbugua, W. 1997. The African Family and the Status of Women's Health. In A. Adepoju (ed.), *Family, Population and Development in Africa*. London and New Jersey: Zed.

Milazi, D. 1998. Migration Within the Context of Poverty and Landlessness in Southern Africa. In Appleyard, R. (ed.), *Emigration Dynamics in Developing Countries, Vol. 1: Sub-Saharan Africa*. Sydney: Ashgate.

MPI (Migration Policy Institute) 2002. Fostering Cooperation between Source and Destination Countries. *Migration Information Source*, October.

Muenz, R. 2006. Europe: Population and Migration in 2005. *Migration Information Source*, June.

Murray, P. 2007. *Profile of UK Diaspora Civil Society Groups involved in International Development – Interests, Attitudes and Involvement: A Mapping Exercise*. London: Connections for Development.

Mutume, G. 2005. Workers' Remittances: A Boon to Development. *Africa Renewal*, 19(3):10.

Netherlands Government 2006. *Towards a Modern Migration Policy*. The Hague: Ministry of Justice.

Newland, K. 2007. A New Surge of Interest in Migration and Development. *Migration Information Source*, February.

OECD (Organisation for Economic Cooperation and Development) 2005. *Trends in International Migration: Annual Report 2004*. Paris: OECD Paris.

—, 2007. *International Migration outlook: Annual report 2007*. Paris: OECD.

Olsen, J., Nordstrom, L. and Corder, M. 2006. Sweden Keeps Doors, Minds Open to Immigrants. *International Herald Tribune (Europe)*. Associated Press, 27 December 2006. http://www.iht.com/articles/ap/2006/12/27/europe/EU_GEN_Welcome_to_Sweden.php (accessed July 2007).

Oppong, C. 1997. African Family Structure and Socio-economic Crisis. In A. Adepoju (ed.), *Family, Population and Development in Africa*. London and New Jersey: Zed.

Orozco, M. 2007. *Remittances and Development: Issues and Policy Opportunities*. Global Forum on Migration and Development: Brussels: Civil Society Day.

Oucho, J.O. 1990. Migrant Linkages in Africa: Retrospect and Prospect. In *The Role of Migration in African Development: Issues and Policies for the '90s*. Commissioned Paper, Union For African Population Studies, Dakar.

—, 1995. Emigration Dynamics of Eastern African Countries. *International Migration*, 33 (3 and 4).

—, 1998. Regional Integration and Labour Mobility in Eastern and Southern Africa. In Appleyard, R. (ed.), *Emigration Dynamics in Developing Countries, Vol. 1: Sub-Saharan Africa*, Sydney: Ashgate.

—, and Crush J. 2001. Contra Free Movement: South Africa and SADC Migration Protocols. *Africa Today*, 48(3):139–158.

Pearson, E. 2002. *Human Traffic, human rights: redefining victim protection*. London: Anti-slavery International.

Ratha, D. 2007. Leveraging remittances for development. *Migration Information Source*.

Ratha, D. and Shaw, W. 2007. *South-South Migration and Remittances*. World Bank Working Paper No. 102. Washington DC: World Bank.

Regional Euro-African Conference "Migration and Development" Rabat 10 July 2006. www.diplomatie.gouv.fr

Report of the Joint Africa-EU Declaration on Migration and Development. Sirte, 22–23 November, 2006. www.africa-union.org/root/au/conferences

Ricca, S. 1989. *International Migration in Africa: Legal and Administrative Aspects*. Geneva: ILO.

RSA (Republic of South Africa) 2004. Department of Health, SA-UK Bilateral Forum Ministerial Meeting, Cape Town, 25 August 2004. www.doh.gov.za/docs/pr/2004/pr0825.html.

—, 2005. Department of Health, Seminar with the UK Health Protection Agency, Pretoria, 21 April 2005. www.info.gov.za/speeches/2005/05042610451002/htm.

Salah, R. 2004. *Child Trafficking: A Challenge to Child Protection in Africa*. Paper presented at the Fourth African Regional Conference on Child Abuse and Neglect. Enugu, March.

SAMP (Southern African Migration Project) (n.d.) http://www.queensu.ca/samp/migrationresources/braindrain/

Sander, C. and Maimbo, S.M. 2003. *Migrant Remittances in Africa: Reducing Obstacles to*

Development Contributions. Africa Region, Working Paper Series No. 64. Washington DC: World Bank.

Scott, M.L., Whelan, A.J., Dewdney, J. and Zwi, A.B. 2004. 'Brain Drain' or Ethical Recruitment? Solving Health Workforce with Professionals from Developing Countries. *Medical Journal of Australia* 180(4):174–76.

Selabe B. 2000. Trafficking in Migration and Forced-Labour in the Southern African Labour Market. Paper presented at Regional Labour Migration Seminar for Southern Africa, Lusaka, 6–9 March.

SID (Society for International Development) 2002. *Declaration of The Hague on the Future of Refugee and Migration Policy.* The Hague: SID Netherlands Chapter.

Sita, N.M. 2003. Trafficking in Women and Children: Situation and Some Trends in African Countries. UNAFRI, May.

Solidar 2007. *Co-development: 'Win-win' Solution for All?* Brussels: Solidar.

Solomon, H. 1997. *Towards the Free Movement of People in Southern Africa?* Institute for Security Studies, Occasional Paper No. 18. Pretoria: Institute for Security Studies.

Sorensen, N.N. 2004. The Development Dimension of Migrant Remittances. *IOM Migration Policy Research Working Paper*, Series No. 1. Geneva: International Organization for Migration.

Stiglitz, J. 2006a. *Making Globalization Work.* New York: Norton.

—, 2006b. *The Tyranny of King Cotton.* Guardian Unlimited: Comment is Free. http://commentisfree.guardian.co.uk/joseph_stiglitz/2006/10/stig.html.

Touré, M. 1998. *Country Report: Côte d'Ivoire.* Regional Meeting of Experts on International Migration in Africa: Trends and Prospects for the 21st Century, Gaborone 2–5 June 1998. UNESCO Network on Migration Research in Africa.

UKNMC (UK Nursing and Midwifery Council) 2005. *Annual Statistics 2004–05.* London: UKNMC.

UN (United Nations) 1996. The United Nations System-wide Special Initiative on Africa. New York: United Nations.

—, 2003. Reversing Africa's 'Brain Drain': New Initiatives Tap Skills of African Expatriates. *Africa Recovery*, 17(2):1.

—, Mixed Results for Regional Economic Blocks. *Africa Renewal*, 18(3):23.

—, 2005. Africa Needs 1 Million Health Professionals. *Africa Renewal*, 18(4):4.

—, 2006a. Africa Confronts Trade Challenges. *Africa Renewal*, 20(1):1.

—, 2006b. African Migration: From Tensions to Solutions. *African Renewal*, 19(4):1.

—, 2007. *Trends in Total Migration Stocks 2005Rrevision.*, POP/DB/MIG/Rev2005. New York: Population Division, Department of Economic and Social Affairs

UNFPA. 2002. *State of World Population 2002: People, poverty and possibilities.* New York: United Nations Population Fund.

—, 2006 *State of World Population 2006: A Passage to Hope – Women and International Migration.* New York: United Nations Population Fund.

UN Habitat 2006. *Urbanization Facts and Figures, 2006.* http://hq.unhabitat.org/mediacentre/documents/wuf2006/WUF%201.pdfconomic

UNICEF 2000. *Child Trafficking in West Africa: Policy Responses.* Florence: UNICEF Innocenti Research Centre.

—, 2003. *Trafficking in Human Beings Especially Women and Children in Africa.* Florence: UNICEF Innocenti Research Centre. http://www.unicef.org/media/files/innocenti_trafficking.doc (accessed July 2007).

Van Agtmael, A. 2007. *The Emerging Markets Century: How a New Breed of World-class Companies is Overtaking the World.* New York: Free Press.

Van Dalen, H.P. and Esveldt, I. 2003. Migratie 'out of Africa'. *Maandschrift Economie*, 67(3):254–65.

Van Moppes, D. 2006. *The African Migration Movement: Routes to Europe.* Working Papers, Migration and Development Series, Report No. 5. Nijmegen: Radboud University.

Veil, L. 1998. The Issue of Child Domestic Labour and Trafficking in West and Central Africa. Report prepared for UNICEF Sub-regional Workshop on Trafficking in Child Domestic Workers, Particularly Girls in Domestic Service, in West and Central Africa Region, Cotonou, 6–8 July.

Westin, C. 2006. Sweden: Restrictive Immigration Policy and Multiculturalism. *Migration Information Source*, June.

Wiltom Park. 2007 *Report of the Wilton Park Conference WP 854 – Human Trafficking: How Best to Stem the Flow?* Wilton Park, UK

Zachariah, K.C. and Condé, J. 1981. *Migration in West Africa: Demographic Aspects.* London: Oxford University Press (with World Bank).

Zlotnik, H. 2003. The Global Dimensions of Female Migration. *Migration Information Source*, March.

CURRENT AFRICAN ISSUES PUBLISHED BY THE INSTITUTE

Recent issues in the series are available electronically
for download free of charge www.nai.uu.se

1. *South Africa, the West and the Frontline States. Report from a Seminar.* 1981, 34 pp, (out-of print)
2. Maja Naur, *Social and Organisational Change in Libya.* 1982, 33 pp, (out-of print)
3. *Peasants and Agricultural Production in Africa. A Nordic Research Seminar. Follow-up Reports and Discussions.* 1981, 34 pp, (out-of print)
4. Ray Bush & S. Kibble, *Destabilisation in Southern Africa, an Overview.* 1985, 48 pp, (out-of print)
5. Bertil Egerö, *Mozambique and the Southern African Struggle for Liberation.* 1985, 29 pp, (out-of print)
6. Carol B.Thompson, *Regional Economic Polic under Crisis Condition. Southern African Development.* 1986, 34 pp, (out-of print)
7. Inge Tvedten, *The War in Angola, Internal Conditions for Peace and Recovery.* 1989, 14 pp, (out-of print)
8. Patrick Wilmot, *Nigeria's Southern Africa Policy 1960–1988.* 1989, 15 pp, (out-of print)
9. Jonathan Baker, *Perestroika for Ethiopia: In Search of the End of the Rainbow?* 1990, 21 pp, (out-of print)
10. Horace Campbell, *The Siege of Cuito Cuanavale.* 1990, 35 pp, (out-of print)
11. Maria Bongartz, *The Civil War in Somalia. Its genesis and dynamics.* 1991, 26 pp, (out-of print)
12. Shadrack B.O. Gutto, *Human and People's Rights in Africa. Myths, Realities and Prospects.* 1991, 26 pp, (out-of print)
13. Said Chikhi, Algeria. *From Mass Rebellion to Workers' Protest.* 1991, 23 pp, (out-of print)
14. Bertil Odén, *Namibia's Economic Links to South Africa.* 1991, 43 pp, (out-of print)
15. Cervenka Zdenek, *African National Congress Meets Eastern Europe. A Dialogue on Common Experiences.* 1992, 49 pp, ISBN 91-7106-337-4, (out-of print)
16. Diallo Garba, *Mauritania–The Other Apartheid?* 1993, 75 pp, ISBN 91-7106-339-0, (out-of print)
17. Zdenek Cervenka and Colin Legum, *Can National Dialogue Break the Power of Terror in Burundi?* 1994, 30 pp, ISBN 91-7106-353-6, (out-of print)
18. Erik Nordberg and Uno Winblad, *Urban Environmental Health and Hygiene in Sub-Saharan Africa.* 1994, 26 pp, ISBN 91-7106-364-1, (out-of print)
19. Chris Dunton and Mai Palmberg, *Human Rights and Homosexuality in Southern Africa.* 1996, 48 pp, ISBN 91-7106-402-8, (out-of print)
20. Georges Nzongola-Ntalaja *From Zaire to the Democratic Republic of the Congo.* 1998, 18 pp, ISBN 91-7106-424-9, (out-of print)
21. Filip Reyntjens, *Talking or Fighting? Political Evolution in Rwanda and Burundi, 1998–1999.* 1999, 27 pp, ISBN 91-7106-454-0, SEK 80.-
22. Herbert Weiss, *War and Peace in the Democratic Republic of the Congo.* 1999, 28 pp, ISBN 91-7106-458-3, SEK 80,-
23. Filip Reyntjens, *Small States in an Unstable Region – Rwanda and Burundi, 1999–2000,* 2000, 24 pp, ISBN 91-7106-463-X, (out-of print)
24. Filip Reyntjens, *Again at the Crossroads: Rwanda and Burundi, 2000–2001.* 2001, 25 pp, ISBN 91-7106-483-4, (out-of print)

25. Henning Melber, *The New African Initiative and the African Union. A Preliminary Assessment and Documentation.* 2001, 36 pp, ISBN 91-7106-486-9, (out-of print)

26. Dahilon Yassin Mohamoda, *Nile Basin Cooperation. A Review of the Literature.* 2003, 39 pp, ISBN 91-7106-512-1, SEK 90,-

27. Henning Melber (ed.), *Media, Public Discourse and Political Contestation in Zimbabwe.* 2004, 39 pp, ISBN 91-7106-534-2, SEK 90,-

28. Georges Nzongola-Ntalaja, *From Zaire to the Democratic Republic of the Congo.* Second and Revised Edition. 2004, 23 pp, ISBN-91-7106-538-5, (out-of print)

29. Henning Melber (ed.), *Trade, Development, Cooperation – What Future for Africa?* 2005, 44 pp, ISBN 91-7106-544-X, SEK 90,-

30. Kaniye S.A. Ebeku, *The Succession of Faure Gnassingbe to the Togolese Presidency – An International Law Perspective.* 2005, 32 pp, ISBN 91-7106-554-7, SEK 90,-

31. Jeffrey V. Lazarus, Catrine Christiansen, Lise Rosendal Østergaard, Lisa Ann Richey, *Models for Life – Advancing antiretroviral therapy in sub-Saharan Africa.* 2005, 33 pp, ISBN 91-7106-556-3, SEK 90,-

32. Charles Manga Fombad and Zein Kebonang, *AU, NEPAD and the APRM – Democratisation Efforts Explored.* Edited by Henning Melber. 2006, 56 pp, ISBN 91-7106-569-5, SEK 90,-

33. Pedro Pinto Leite, Claes Olsson, Magnus Schöldtz, Toby Shelley, Pål Wrange, Hans Corell and Karin Scheele, *The Western Sahara Conflict – The Role of Natural Resources in Decolonization.* Edited by Claes Olsson. 2006, 32 pp, ISBN 91-7106-571-7, SEK 90,-

34. Jassey, Katja and Stella Nyanzi, *How to Be a "Proper" Woman in the Times of HIV and AIDS.* 2007, 35 pp, ISBN 91-7106-574-1, SEK 90,-

35. Lee, Margaret, Henning Melber, Sanusha Naidu and Ian Taylor, *China in Africa.* Compiled by Henning Melber. 2007, 47 pp, ISBN 978-91-7106-589-6, SEK 90,-

36. Nathaniel King, *Conflict as Integration. Youth Aspiration to Personhood in the Teleology of Sierra Leone's 'Senseless War'.* 2007, 32 pp, ISBN 978-91-7106-604-6, SEK 90,-

37. Aderanti Adepoju, *Migration in sub-Saharan Africa.* 2008. 70 pp, ISBN 978-91-7106-620-6

www.ingramcontent.com/pod-product-compliance
Ingram Content Group UK Ltd.
Pitfield, Milton Keynes, MK11 3LW, UK
UKHW051251180426
11947UKWH00020B/1663